The Deaf Way II Anthology

A Literary Collection by Deaf and Hard of Hearing Writers

Tonya M. Stremlau, *Editor*

D1115615

Gallaudet University Press   *Washington, D.C.*

Gallaudet University Press
Washington, DC 20002
http://gupress.gallaudet.edu

The Deaf Way II Anthology was created as part of the Deaf Way II International Conference and Arts Festival hosted by Gallaudet University in Washington, D.C., in July 2002.

This book is supported in part by an award from the National Endowment for the Arts.

"The Hands of My Father" by Christopher Heuer was previously published in *Kaleidoscope: Exploring the Experience of Disability through Literature and the Fine Arts*, 44 (winter/spring 2002): 61. Kaleidoscope Press, 701 Main St., Akron, Ohio 44311-1019.

"How to Become a Backstabber" and "Depths of the River" by Raymond Luczak © 2001 by Raymond Luczak.

"Every Man Must Fall" by Willy Conley © 2000 by Willy Conley.

Cover and interior design by Dennis Anderson

Front cover illustration: *Spring Root* by Iris Aranda; oil on canvas

Back cover photograph: *After the Rain* by Rita Straubhaar

Library of Congress Cataloging-in-Publication Data

The deaf way II anthology : a literary collection by deaf and hard of hearing writers / Tonya M. Stremlau, editor.
    p. cm.
  ISBN 1-56368-127-7
    1. Deaf, Writings of the, American. 2. Hearing impaired, Writings of the, American. 3. Hearing impaired—Literary collections. 4. Deaf—Literary collections. 5. American literature—20th century. I. Title: Deaf way 2 anthology. II. Title: Deaf way two anthology. III. Stremlau, Tonya M.

PS508.D43 D43 2002
810.8'9208162—dc21

                          2002023502

Contents

Introduction

JOHN KITTO, who was deafened by a fall at the age of twelve, wrote in his 1848 autobiography, *The Lost Senses*, that "the nature of my affliction [deafness] unfitted me for any other sphere of usefulness than that of literature" (218).[1] Kitto explains that he made the decision to write because it was something he could do alone, without having to communicate in the frustrating world of hearing people. However, he points out that deaf writers have special difficulties because the profession "involves, or should involve, intimacy with men of similar pursuits" (219). Kitto had no fellow deaf writers with whom to form a community of peers. He had hearing literary friends but, not surprisingly, found communication with them limited and difficult.

It is easier today for a deaf writer to find peers; many more people are writing than are included in this anthology. The writers represented here submitted their work for the cultural arts festival of Deaf Way II in July 2002. This international festival, hosted by Gallaudet University in Washington, D.C., provided a rare opportunity for deaf writers to discuss their art. It might seem unsurprising to include literary arts in a cultural festival, but, in the deaf world, the visual arts—including signed language performances—are central to cultural identity whereas the written ones are not.

"Deaf writer" still seems something of an oddity in the deaf community. Writing, after all, is produced in the language of schools of the oppressive hearing culture. Deaf people, not being able to hear, do not acquire language through listening. The only real way for deaf people to acquire and build on the language knowledge necessary for reading and writing is through the

---

1. John Kitto, "The Lost Senses," in *Angels and Outcasts: An Anthology of Deaf Characters in Literature*, 3d ed., ed. Trent Batson and Eugene Bergman (Washington, D.C.: Gallaudet University Press, 1985), 209-60.

written word. Deaf children cannot overhear a new word while waiting in line at the grocery store or in parents' incidental conversations.

On the other hand, the deaf community has an important written element to its culture—newspapers. Printing is one of the trades for which deaf students trained in school, and that helped create a rich tradition of newspapers produced by and for members of the deaf community. That, of course, means many deaf people were writing articles and columns. Yet somehow this has not translated into an awareness of deaf people as writers, not even in the deaf community. In my job as a professor in the Gallaudet University English department, I have had students insist to me that they could not possibly be expected to use English well because they were deaf.

Therefore, one important reason to publish this collection is to raise awareness in both the deaf and hearing communities that deaf people do write. Another is to show how deaf writers portray deaf characters and deaf experiences. I was always a voracious reader. After I became deaf when I was ten, I became very aware of how rarely I ran into deaf characters. They were so few that I remember each one: Mr. Singer in Carson McCullers' *The Heart Is a Lonely Hunter*; Albert and Ellie in Eudora Welty's "The Key"; Donald in Shel Silverstein's "Deaf Donald"; and Will Barrett (hard of hearing) in Walker Percy's *The Last Gentleman* and *The Second Coming*. The only deaf writer I read (or knew about) was Helen Keller.

Finally I decided to go looking for deaf writers on my own. I knew there had to be some. I started with autobiographies and memoirs, since that is what I found: Bernard Bragg's *Lessons in Laughter*, Henry Kisor's *What's That Pig Outdoor*s and Leo Jacobs's *A Deaf Adult Speaks Out* were the first three I read. There were many differences in the three—especially Kisor from Bragg and Jacobs because Kisor is not a member of the deaf community while the other two are—but with all three I found myself identifying strongly with their experiences. Even when their experiences differed from mine I felt connected because the descriptions of their experiences as deaf people rang true.

When I finally found deaf writers who wrote poetry, drama, or fiction about deaf experiences, I felt a similar connection. A good example is Willy Conley's play, *The Hearing Test*. The deaf character, Michael, isn't much like me—he's prelingually deaf and wears a hearing aid, and is a guy as well. But I do know how claustrophobic a soundproof hearing test booth is. I know how ridiculous it feels to take a hearing test that will just tell me the same old news—duh, I can't hear. I know how boring and uncomfortable it is to sit with heavy earphones on, waiting to raise my arm when I hear a sound in my ear, but it never comes and all I feel is a buzzing against my head. Thus, at the end of the play, when Michael cut the plug off the radio cord in the audiologist's waiting room, I felt vicarious revenge against all the audiologists in my life who tortured me with their good intentions.

The authenticity with which deaf writers portray the deaf experience makes reading them an ideal way for hearing people to develop a better understanding of what it is like to be deaf. Not that a hearing writer cannot create realistic, sympathetic deaf characters. Hearing writers, though, can only imagine what it must be like not to hear, and they have to try to put aside their hearing biases. Perhaps the most famous modern deaf character in literature is Sarah, the central character in Mark Medoff's *Children of a Lesser God*. Sarah is strong and smart, but she also stays in a menial job at her former school until she is "rescued" by James, the hearing speech teacher. Even the title of the play (although it can be interpreted in other ways) seems to say that deaf people are a lesser creation of an inferior god. I cannot imagine a deaf writer giving this title to a play about deaf people.

The writers in this anthology have many different things to say about life as a deaf person, yet their experiences are common to deaf people everywhere. They tell of being isolated at (hearing) family dinners or of not knowing what is announced over a public address system. They tell of what it is like to be a deaf writer, including dealing with expectations that they can't write because they are deaf. If you do not know much about deaf people or deaf culture, reading this anthology is a good way to start. And for those who are familiar with deaf culture, the works collected here bring the deaf experience to life as literature.

Of course, deaf writers do not write about deaf-related things only, nor should they, since being deaf is only one aspect of a deaf writer's life. In this anthology you will find works about beauty, love, racism, word play, and. . . . Well, you can read on to find out.

—Tonya Marie Stremlau

The Deaf Way II Anthology would not have been possible without the assistance of the many reviewers who gave generously of their time to read submissions and provide recommendations. Special thanks go to Pia Seagrave, who provided guidance in the first phases of this project; to Harvey Goodstein, Jay Innes, Tim McCarty, Paul Harrelson, and Lijiao Huang from Deaf Way II; and Ivey Pittle Wallace from Gallaudet University Press.

The Deaf Way II Anthology

Curtis Robbins

CURTIS ROBBINS is a published poet and an educator. He has been teaching computer applications and American Sign Language for almost 35 years. Robbins became deaf at the age of one from the side effects of a drug he was given to treat tonsillitis. He attended public schools in New York City and Long Island, and graduated from Gallaudet University in 1967. He earned his masters degrees from New York University and the University of Maryland, where he also earned his Ph.D. Robbins lives with his wife and two children in Maryland.

No Rhythm, They Say

Some people say
        because I'm deaf
                I've no rhythm.

I might confess to that
              but then I shan't
        out of the misnomer in the logic
                  about rhythm.

Why, don't you know
        that everything we do
              in life is done in the rhythm?

Does it matter whether you hear it or not?

Now, of course, it's not by
              the beat of the drum --
        not every be-bobbing dum-dee-dum
        is in the rhythm --
    it takes a sound mind
        to imbibe and imbue
              with rhythm.

Once I get the knack
        of doing something right,
           the logic of the action
                concludes the intent
                  of the rhythm.

That's logically sound, yes?

And so, it takes rhythm —
        there's nothing
    my mind wouldn't hear
      that rings
           the twangs of Silence's rhythm.

Empty Ears

Consider the ear
shaped like the bass clef
but empty.

"We Come to Silence," Linda Pastan

The musicale
of my environs

     is not
    the wrath
    of my ears

         nor
        silence
        in
       my eyes.

Solo Dining While Growing Up

When my whole family sat down at the dinner table:

There was always
                  a lot to eat from corner to corner

There was always conversation
                between forks and spoons

There was always conversation
                between glasses and cups

There was always conversation
                between napkins

There were always
                empty plates and empty bowls

But the knife that laid between them all —
                from mouth to ear —
                      from mouth to eye —

                                  cut me off.

Learning Up Front

For as long as I remember

I've always

I sat up front of the class

so I could watch Teacher

otherwise I'd be sitting

in the back somewhere

reading lips

between bobbing, swaying, nodding heads:

some were tall

some were fat

some had perms wide or high

some had bushy ducktails or ponytails

some even had crewcuts

that the rest didn't matter

As long as I sat up front

so I could watch Teacher.

Some teachers

talked chalkpoking the blackboard

Some teachers

talked flipping fanning pages

Some teachers

talked zigzagging rows of aisles

that bobbing, swaying, nodding

heads didn't matter

As long as I sat up front

so I could watch Teacher.

When my classmates spoke
        I never knew who
as long as I sat up front
        so I could watch Teacher.

Whether meticulously copious notes were
        written on the blackboard or
        on blue on white
        nauseating ammoniated ditto or
        on black on white
        ink-blotted, letter-smudged
        mimeograph or
        read from the book

As long as I sat up front
        so I could watch Teacher.

Never once could I tell
        how much I understood —
        a day never went
        without daydreams --
it never really mattered
        as long as I sat up front
        so I could watch Teacher.

About the Tale of an Old Bay Fisherman

Have you ever gone
     someplace near the Bay
       and tried sitting by a grumpy,
         whiskered,
           whiskey-nosed,
             lispy lipping leper
         of an old, reddened,
      sunbaked,
        waveslapped,
         windsogged,
           thick-skinned fisherman
       from those windjamming days
        amid the odorous
     decaying deadfish, seafresh air
  listening to the tales
     of crab grabbing, oyster hoist-raking days
          with gazing agape,
            with mesmeric awe —
     thunderstruck by his filthy
       weather-worn,
         yellow-stemmed,
      fierce-looking face-carved,
          blackened white
       meerschaum pipe
clenched between his tobacco-stained,
    shellcracked,
      rope-battened teeth —
       shucking bluefins and
         occasional oysters
       with rapid sleight
     of water-thickened,
    short-stumped,
   fat-fingered,
  bare hands?

No, I wouldn't have —
  I wouldn't be able to lipread him.

Hand Tied

How does a Deaf poet indite
        and end up with unintended umlauts
            of which mispronunciations
                are unheard of
                    especially if not
                        recited by hand?

But how could a Deaf poet
        end up with
            a written commotion
                as chaotic
                    as a metric foot
                        in his mouth?

As if sound is by rote
        assonant by assimilation
            of which pronunciations
                are deftly arresting
                    by umlauts
                      by insinuendo.

Melissa Whalen

MELISSA WHALEN attended Smith College in Northampton, Massachusetts, and spent her junior year abroad at the University of Bristol in England, studying British Sign Language, Deaf culture, and sociolinguistics. She graduated magna cum laude from Smith, with a major in sociology and a minor in women's studies, and was admitted to Phi Beta Kappa. After graduation, Whalen received a Fulbright scholarship to study at La Trobe University in Melbourne, Australia, where she earned a masters degree in Australian Sign Language Linguistics. Currently, Whalen is working with the National Association of the Deaf as a project specialist for the National Council on Interpreting. The essays included in this anthology were written while she lived in Australia.

The Noisy House

I CREPT SLOWLY out of bed and glanced at the clock on my bed-side table. The bright green numbers glowed as I whispered "4: 16 a.m." to myself. The house was being noisy again tonight and I had to figure out why. I couldn't sleep because of the noise. Mom and Dad didn't believe me. They couldn't hear the noises. They just told me, "You're Deaf, sweetie. You must be imagining things. There are no noises." Dad would walk me back to bed and tuck me in, and five minutes later, the house would become noisy again. This time, I wouldn't go to them. Even at seven years old, I knew that I wasn't imagining things. I would figure it out alone.

Determined, I tiptoed out of my bedroom and down the hall to the kitchen. I stood next to the refrigerator and listened as hard as I could. I knew it sometimes made noise, but it was quiet tonight. I tried the dishwasher, the coffeepot, and the toilet in turn before I decided the noise wasn't coming from the kitchen. So I made my way down to the basement and leaned against the furnace. There was no noise. In fact, the noises I had earlier heard had disappeared. But I knew they were there. They'd come back to taunt me the minute I climbed in bed.

"What else makes noise?" I wondered silently. The house was very dark and very quiet just then, and I had never been awake so late at night. I started to become a bit frightened. Trying to shake it off, I moved into the family room and checked the stereo and the radio. I crawled back up the dark stairs and checked both doors to make sure they were locked. I listened outside my little sister's bedroom to see if she'd left some hearing toy on. Nothing. Finally, out of desperation, I opened the door to my parent's bedroom and stumbled around to my mother's side of the bed. "Mom," I whispered, "I can't find the noises. They will come back when I get into bed."

"Oh, sweetie," mumbled my mother, "there are no noises. You just had a nightmare. Don't worry; Daddy will tuck you in again." She reached over and shook my father by the shoulder, saying, "Take Melissa back to bed," as she rolled over again.

"No!" I said angrily, on the verge of tears. "You never listen to me!" I ran out of the room and climbed into bed on my own. When my father arrived to tuck in the blankets, I pretended to be asleep. As soon as he left, I opened my eyes and waited. Sure enough, the noises were back. I started to cry from frustration and stuck my fingers deep into my ears. It didn't work. I could still hear the noises clearly.

Suddenly, a thought hit me. At school, when I put my fingers in my ears, the classroom seemed quieter. I could block out some of the confusing background noise that made no sense to me. Yet, these noises couldn't be blocked out. Perhaps Mom was right when she said they were in my head. It was such a novel idea to me. I played with it for awhile. If the noises were in my head, then I wasn't crazy. I wasn't really imagining things; my head was just noisier than most people's were. This made sense to me. After all, I was Deaf. Probably Deaf people had a lot of strange noises in their heads that hearing people couldn't understand. I fell asleep puzzling over my new theory.

Eventually, I came to realize that a lot of the things I thought I heard were coming from inside my head. So I developed a system of my own. If I couldn't identify the source of a strange noise, and none of the hearing people in the vicinity seemed bothered, I stuck my fingers in my ears. Noises that continued even though my fingers were pushed as far as they could go into my ears were labeled "head noises." I quickly learned to do these "tests" in secret so as not to appear ridiculous. After all, I reasoned, how odd it would seem to see a seven-year-old Deaf child with her fingers stuck into her ears.

Nine years later, at the age of sixteen, I transferred to a residential school for Deaf students. During a required Deaf history class, I came across an article entitled "Tinnitus: The Battle against Head Noise." Suddenly it all fell into place. I wasn't crazy, and I wasn't alone.

The article said that many Deaf people suffered from tinnitus, which is most commonly characterized by ringing or buzzing noises in one's head. I asked around and found out that my roommate even heard songs repeated over and over in her head. "Happy Birthday" would play for weeks on end. Other classmates heard high-pitched squeals, bell-like sounds, or just general static-like noises. Indeed, the article claimed that 10 percent of the hearing population suffers from tinnitus as well. It has no known cure, but is often brought on by ear damage after overexposure to loud noises. Ironically, several theories suggest that forcing Deaf children to wear hearing aids set to inappropriately high levels may lead to tinnitus later in life.

I read the article several times. "Tinnitus," I thought. So it had a name. I remembered all those visits to the audiologist, when I would raise my hand to indicate that I heard nonexistent noises. "I haven't started the test yet," the audiologist would tell me. "But I hear things," I always replied. No one seemed to understand that when it was quiet in my environment, the noises in my head took over. At times, I thought I might be going crazy.

It was a small thing, really, in the grand scheme of things, I thought to myself. My childhood did not suffer radically because I was forced to invent strange games for determining the etiology of noises. Still, I felt like jumping for joy that day in class because I had discovered a simple medical fact that cleared up so much confusion. And yet, I also felt like crying. How many other Deaf children out there, I wondered, had to go through exactly the same thing? Why do we have to reinvent the wheel a thousand different ways? Why didn't people listen to us? Why didn't my parents listen to me? It's not right—that second graders should end up wandering around dark houses at night searching for phantom noises.

It could have been so simple. If only someone in authority had told them about the increased likelihood that their Deaf daughter might experience tinnitus. If only they had known how to explain to me the difference between real noises and noises inside my head. I could have gotten much more sleep and spent a lot less time in strange corners with my fingers stuck in my ears.

The information about tinnitus exists, but it lives mainly inside medical journals and other academic publications—certainly not the types of books that most parents are apt to read. The general public has very little knowledge about the prevalence of tinnitus among Deaf children and adults. And even less understanding about the day-to-day realities of a young Deaf child's world. Despite the army of psychologists, special education teachers, speech therapists, audiologists, and the numerous other "experts" on the problem of Deafness, the fact remains: Only those who have been there really know what it is like. And today, there are still far too few Deaf adults willing or able to tell it like it is. An inadequate educational system, lack of encouragement, and unfamiliarity with the written English language combine to discourage Deaf adults from sharing their childhood thoughts and feelings with the world.

This is my attempt to remedy that. I want future parents to know how to explain such situations to their Deaf children. I want all people who work with Deaf children to have at least a better glimpse of the myriad strategies they invent to make sense of an overwhelming world. Armed with this information, and with a deeper understanding of their world, parents can offer their Deaf children the chance to be just that—children.

Oil and Straw

EVERY AMERICAN who attended public school will remember one of the most enduring morning rituals in our nation's classrooms— the Pledge of Allegiance. Every morning, thousands of children all across America stand up, face the flag, and place their hands over their heart. More or less in unison, they mumble the Pledge of Allegiance to the United States of America and then promptly fall back into their seats.

I was no exception. On my first day of school, I was taught the words to this important ritual. Or rather, my class was taught the words. Being Deaf, I missed quite a lot of the lesson. As a result, I spent the next six years mumbling an odd assortment of words. My morning ritual went something like this:

"I pledge allegiance to the flag of the United States of America. And to . . . re pubclick . . . for witches stands . . . one vacation, under God, in division, with liberty and oil and straw."

This may sound quite bizarre, but to me, it made sense in its own way. After all, many things about the hearing world were bizarre. I was only five years old when I started school, and the morning recital happened so predictably that the words took on a life of their own. For many years, I am sure I really believed that my classmates recited the same thing I did. Being a highly creative child, I could see the connections between witches, oil, straw, burning flags, and God. Since I spoke so softly, no one ever heard me well enough to correct me.

When I became old enough to realize that my recitation made no sense at all, it was too late. I couldn't admit to anyone that I was ten years old and had been mumbling rubbish every morning for six years. My stubborn pride wouldn't allow it. So I stood at attention still, but from then on, I refused to say anything beyond the first sentence. They never took the time to teach me properly, I reasoned. Why should I make myself look like a fool by spouting nonsense about oil and straw? Two years later, at the age of twelve, I finally came across the real words in a textbook. Still, this didn't do much to diminish the fire of anger that was building within me.

In many ways, this realization was part of a rude awakening on my part. I began to look around at my life. I became aware of all the songs to which I sang the wrong words, all the little rituals whose significance passed me by, and all the stories and rhymes that I had misinterpreted over the years. I woke up one morning and, suddenly, I couldn't trust myself any more. I couldn't trust my own memory or the things I thought I knew because I kept turning out to be wrong. I felt like my past had become a bed of quicksand.

And I was angry with "them." Because they told me that I was a success and that I did a beautiful job of fitting into the hearing world. "I keep forgetting that you're Deaf," said my teachers. "You seem just like the other students." "And you speak so well, if a bit softly," said my parents. "We're so proud of you."

"But I'm not just like them," I wanted to shout. "You lied. You taught me that if I seemed to fit in well, that was good enough." That became my goal. Who cared if I didn't know the Pledge of Allegiance or if I sang all the wrong words to Christmas carols? It's all right, I told myself, if I didn't know the names of half my classmates by the end of the year. Because I was a success. I got all A's in school. I beat those hearing classmates. I believed in myself, and I believed that I had a handle on things—the best handle I could ever expect to have.

And then all of sudden, I realized that I didn't have life figured out all that well. My superior oral skills and lipreading abilities just didn't give me anywhere near complete access to the world around me. It seemed like all the people I had trusted for so many years to look after my best interests had suddenly been revealed as members of the opposing team. It took a long time for me to let go of that anger and to accept that my parents had simply done what they thought best for me at the time, based upon their view of the world. Perhaps the most important thing I learned in those turbulent teenage years, however, is that their worldview did not have to be mine. I learned how to "shift my center."

Shifting the Center

DURING MY middle teenage years, my parents tried mightily to get me into speech therapy. I fought back with everything I had, and my sassiness soon became too much for the school therapist. All efforts to improve my speech were abandoned. I was thirteen years old and I absolutely refused to be "different" in any way. Besides, I could still understand some of my teachers, even with a progressive hearing loss bordering on profound, and I had a few close friends. It was enough for me then.

Two years later, things were not quite as happy. At fifteen, I could no longer follow classes at all and had resorted to reading fiction novels under the desk. I still got all A's, but my old friends had long since moved on to weekend dates with boyfriends and female friends willing to go out at night. I had somehow lost all my friends. I couldn't bear joining a group only to have my communication inadequacies made vividly clear, and I couldn't figure any way out of what seemed like a hopeless situation. I fell into a deep clinical depression that lasted over a year.

Thus, in my sophomore year of high school, my parents seized upon the idea of speech therapy again. Perhaps they thought that improving my speech would solve some of my problems. Since none of us really discussed my unhappiness and no one knew what to do about it anyway, I gave in to their wishes and agreed to spend half an hour every Monday with the school speech therapist. I insisted that our sessions take place after school hours so that no one would see me there.

To my surprise, I loved speech therapy. Oh, the actual lessons themselves were a waste of time. My habits were set and I wasn't going to stand in front of the mirror for hours practicing "k" sounds. I was intelligent enough to know that my speech wasn't the problem. Instead, I made a note of which sounds I couldn't pronounce correctly and from then on, remembered to choose words to use with unfamiliar hearing people that I knew were clear and easily understood. I learned how to say, for instance, "Gary, with a G as in garage," so that I didn't get the response, "I'm sorry, there's no Terry here."

Such lessons, however, took up only a small portion of my time with the therapist, Sarah. The rest of the time, we talked. Sarah was young and easily distracted, and she was fascinated with me. She'd never met an accomplished Deaf person before. She wanted to know about my life, about my opinions on things, and about how I survived in a hearing school with no interpreter. Sarah praised my speech over and over, telling me how clearly I spoke for someone with such a profound hearing loss. She listened to me when I talked, and she didn't correct my speech or my pronunciation outside of the specific exercises we did together.

I began to look forward to Mondays. Sometimes, Sarah would be the first person I spoke to all day because my depression caused me to drift silently through each class, and my teachers allowed it. Sarah was interested in me, I realized, as a Deaf teenager. She made me feel alive in a way that no one else could. And I couldn't quite put it into words, but I knew she was something special. So I practiced "s" sounds with my teeth closed just to make her happy and tried to figure out why I was willing to do this.

And one day, out of the blue, I understood. Sarah approached me from a different "center." She saw my strengths as a Deaf person, even though I didn't yet identify as such. She compared my speech to my Deaf peers, not to the speech abilities of the hearing people all around me. She tried to teach me to talk more clearly, yes, because that was her job, but she didn't try all that hard. Perhaps she understood that at that point in my life, I needed a friend more than I needed to speak perfectly.

The summer before my junior year of high school began, I informed my parents I would be moving to a residential Deaf school in Washington D.C. They weren't really given much choice in the matter. I figured that having hit rock bottom emotionally gave me a lot more say when it came to decisions about my future. After all, I hadn't seen any brilliant solutions from their end, so I took matters into my own hands. Before I left, I wrote a letter to Sarah to say goodbye. I let my parents read the draft. I didn't have the courage to say it out loud, but I could let them read my feelings on paper.

The last paragraph of the letter read, "Thank you for seeing me as a capable Deaf person with better than average speech, rather than a hearing-impaired person with faulty speech. Thank you for being able to see me from a different center, from a different perspective, and for allowing me the chance to view myself through your eyes. I liked the person I saw there, but I don't like who I am now. So I am going away to school. Whatever happens, I will always remember you for your friendship and the gift you gave me—the realization that I've been unfairly comparing myself to people who are not my peers. You did a lousy job of fixing my speech, Sarah, but a magnificent job of being my friend. Thank you."

Sarah may have been the first person to see me from a different center, but she was not the last. After I learned the language of my Deaf classmates, I came to realize that all of Deaf culture is based upon this same notion—a "center" in which Deafness is taken as the norm. As I grew more self-confident and developed pride in who I was, I dragged my family along on an exhilarating journey. I was determined to discover everything I felt I'd missed out on in the hearing world. In doing so, I forced those I loved to radically change their ideas about what it means to be Deaf.

Friendly Trees

When I was a very small child, music was a wonderful part of my life. I sang in the school choir, dressed in my little plaid skirt, and standing in the front row. I always made sure that I sat in the very front of the room for music class so that I could lipread the instructor. Of course, I was not like all other Deaf children. I was born hearing and began to lose it around the age of two, so that during primary school, sound and music were still accessible to me via the normal channels.

I was also fortunate to have a marvelously dedicated mother. She couldn't sing in tune to save her life, but she would spend hours with me helping me to learn the words to the fifth-grade school play. We must have spent over fifty hours together sitting by the tape player on my bedroom floor singing, "When it rains, it rains pennies from heaven." We devised a whole host of clever tricks to enable me to fully participate in a two-hour singing production involving one hundred children and twenty songs. I don't think I ever properly thanked her for the time she gave me.

But by the time middle school rolled around, music began to take on ugly associations in my life. I didn't listen to the radio as it made no sense to me, and I didn't know the famous rock stars of the times. I was shut out of my classmates' discussions about popular music. I had no crushes on male singing heartthrobs. And choir became a group of children chosen based on real talent, not simply blind enthusiasm. I no longer had access to music in my daily life. I began to hate everything associated with music and the hearing people who so enjoyed it.

Then, when I was sixteen years old, I transferred to a Deaf school and joined a Deaf theater troupe that performed all over the world. The Road Show, as it was called, translated songs, poems, and skits into American Sign Language and performed in schools, churches, and clubs all over the country, as well as overseas during our summer tours. Suddenly, music became accessible again. Or rather, I came to understand that it always had been accessible. I simply didn't know how to enjoy it until I arrived, ironically, at a Deaf school.

The Road Show practiced eight hours a week in the school auditorium. We had an excellent sound system, with speakers set up to send the music both out into the audience and onto the stage for the performers. We cranked up that stereo and let the music blast. Along with thirteen other Deaf teenagers, I jumped, danced, sang, and signed music just as enthusiastically as any hearing sixteen-year-old. With the music cranked up loud, I found that I could follow along. I just needed to memorize the words first. And if I couldn't hear a particular song, it didn't matter. We all learned to memorize our cues and to coordinate the dances together. The audiences never had a clue which of us were totally Deaf and which could hear the lyrics. Like I said, it didn't matter. We all enjoyed the music, and we all learned what it meant to be professional performers.

I had finally found something that I was really good at; I liked the stage, and the stage liked me. I came alive under those spotlights. I would sign beautiful ASL translations of songs and mouth the English words silently to myself. It was a revelation for me and for those who loved me. Music was once again a part of my daily life.

However, because my lip patterns were exceptionally clear, I often got myself into trouble. My friends have labeled the most hilarious of these episodes the "friendly tree" story. A song that we were performing had already been translated into ASL by previous generations of performers. It was taught to me in ASL and because I did not know the English lyrics, I added my own lip patterns to the signing. This resulted in me "singing" the comical expression: "where friendly trees." After three rehearsals, the director finally sat me down and said "Mel, if you insist on moving your mouth so much, you MUST use the English lyrics." The real sentence read "in a grove of shady trees." The troupe burst out in laughter and from that day on, I never stopped hearing about the "friendly trees."

The "friendly trees" is more than just a funny story, though. It also marked a turning point in my relationship with music and with the hearing world at large. I had finally found people who accepted both sides of me: the Deaf teenager who had so recently discovered the beauty of ASL and the hearing side of me that wanted to use my native English. The Road Show accepted my desire to "sing" in English and it taught me how to translate those lyrics into beautiful, visual ASL songs that were accessible to a Deaf audience. I was not forced to give up anything. Instead, I discovered a new joy in life.

When I went home for Christmas that year, I asked for a portable CD player. I spent much of that winter break locked in my room with the headphones on and my CD player blasting. My parents learned to check for written lyrics before they bought me a new CD. And occasionally, one of them would sit on the floor with me and sing along to the music so that I could memorize the breaks and pauses of the singer. This helped me follow the song on my own immeasurably.

They were a little shocked, I am sure. They sent a Deaf daughter away to a residential Deaf school because she hated life in a hearing school, and she came home and locked herself in her bedroom with a CD player just like their younger teenager. I am sure they found the whole phenomena quite ironic. Yet, they encouraged me. My mother bought me all the CDs she'd never bought before. My father discussed country music with me. Both of them tolerated it when I turned up the country music channel on the television so loud that the walls of the house echoed with "my achy-breaky heart."

Between the friendly trees and the achy-breaky hearts, I came to realize that music was not the exclusive province of the hearing world. I did not need to be excluded. I simply needed to change the rules. And my parents agreed. Together, we wondered why, in all those years of mainstreaming, we had never thought about other ways to make music enjoyable for me. Perhaps because those who approach the world with one set of perceptions have a hard time creating alternative strategies for those with a different experience of the world.

At the Deaf school, we had a special music room in which flashing colored lights represented the different musical tones. When the stereo was turned on, the room became a disco, a kaleidoscope of colors flashing around the walls. It was a joy to behold. Obviously, rooms such as that one are few. But music itself is not. And creativity is certainly not in short supply in this world.

Perhaps the most precious gift that parents can give a young Deaf child is the sense that there are no limits. They can convey the message that music, just like everything else in this world, is for everyone. We may all experience it differently, but each individual's understanding of music is unique and valuable. When I learned that music did not have to be a source of pain and exclusion, I let go of a lot of my anger. I began to see that the isolation I had experienced was based more on ignorance than on any genuine desire to exclude me. As my anger faded, I became more open to talking about music, to sharing lyrics with friends, and even to singing in the shower. Today, as an adult, I waste an awful lot of water practicing my "low voice" but I enjoy every minute of it.

Ariana

EVERY SUMMER, since I was seventeen years old, I've worked at the Michigan Womyn's Music Festival for several weeks. One year, I was assigned to the day care center that looked after the children of other workers during the time it took to set-up, run, and dismantle the festival. That summer, one of our youngest charges was Deaf.

Her name was Ariana, and she came from Venezuela. Her

mother was also Deaf, so she had the benefit of sign language in the home. However, Ariana had not been adopted until she was three years old. Thus, for the first three years of her life, she had no way to communicate. Her language was considerably delayed for her age.

Ariana used physicality to compensate for her still-developing language. Unfortunately for her, the other six-, seven-, and eight-year-old children weren't too keen on being shoved around playfully. One day, the group, which was composed solely of girls, gathered in one corner of the playroom and refused to interact with her. They knew a bit of sign language, but that made no difference. None of my explanations, entreaties, or demands could convince them to include Ariana in their play. Their games were verbal and her roughness had no place in them. And because they knew how badly I wanted her included, they saw a golden opportunity to extract revenge for the excessive amount of time I spent with Ariana. When she approached them, they ran away. They made faces at her, and my punishments had no effect. Nothing worked.

I stopped trying to force inclusion, and Ariana gave up and curled herself into a ball in the play crib we kept for the toddlers. She could barely fit, but somehow she managed, and she would not respond to my offers to play with her. With my teeth clamped tightly shut and my breathing controlled, I managed to make it through the rest of my shift alone. As soon as it was over, I said goodbye to Ariana, still curled up silently in her crib, and raced back to my tent. My tentmate arrived later that evening to find me sobbing uncontrollably. Her consoling comment that, "they're only being children" did nothing to calm my sobs. That was the problem—they were only being children. And children can be very cruel.

When I looked at Ariana, I saw myself. I saw a four-year-old version of myself watching the neighborhood children rush headlong out of the house when my back was turned slightly, laughing wildly at their ability to "fool" me. I heard the incessant shouts of

"CAN YOU HEAR ME?" directed at my back on the playgrounds of my childhood. I remembered the children who got up and moved away from lunch tables when I sat down, whispering behind cupped hands as they left.

I couldn't handle watching Ariana go through the same thing. Yet, I knew I couldn't protect her any more than my mother could protect me when I had been her age. When I was small and the children hurt me, my mother sat down beside me and said, "Don't worry, I'll color with you." But I hadn't wanted her sympathy then any more than Ariana wanted mine that day.

That night in my tent, I realized that I had never properly expressed any of my own grief, tears, and frustration. The children's behavior had triggered a switch worthy of many hours of therapy. But since I didn't have the money to pay for those hours of lying on a warm, accepting couch, I would have to learn to deal with the memories on my own. The first step, I decided, would be to think about ways in which parents could help their own Deaf children deal with such situations.

We can't protect Deaf children, no, but we can make it easier sometimes. We can explain why other children are frightened of differences. We can talk to them about why their Deafness confuses their classmates, and ask the school to provide training workshops for both students and staff. These things will not eliminate all of the teasing, but they will help. And when children are cruel, we can be honest. We can tell our Deaf children, "Yes, sometimes people are cruel." For all children, both hearing and Deaf recognize that this is a part of reality. Denying the truth robs them of the respect they deserve. "I'll play with you" not only doesn't help, but it also reinforces the belief that Mom and Dad really don't understand if they think that their company will compensate for peer rejection. We cannot protect the Arianas of the world, but we can show them that we know their feelings are real and as worthy of respect as those of anyone else. Sometimes simple recognition can be the hardest thing to do, but it is the best approach.

Tell It Like It Is

THESE ARE some of the most vivid memories of my childhood. Some are sad, some are quite funny, and some bring smiles of joy to my face. All, I hope, are educational in their own way. As I recount them, I am reminded that I am not as unique as I would often like to believe. In my travels as an adult, I have met a great many other Deaf adults who were once Deaf children. And they have told me stories about their own noisy houses, botched versions of the Pledge of Allegiance, and the joys of finding a community of Deaf people who appreciate friendly trees. Those who dragged their families along for the ride have invariably also managed to become closer to loved ones as they learned how to better love themselves.

I have presented these episodes in roughly chronological order, to give readers a better sense of the shape of my life thus far. Each of the stories focuses on a turning point in my life, while inviting parents of Deaf children to take from it what they may. I will not lie and say that I have no political agenda, for I think my perspective is very clear in this mini-autobiography; I strongly urge all parents of Deaf children to explore Deaf culture with their children while they are young.

But my purpose here goes beyond simply continuing the endless debate over language choice for Deaf children. I want all people who come into contact with Deaf children to have a deeper understanding of the range of strategies they employ as they struggle to make sense of a world that still does not value their unique difference. The experiences of Deaf children and their interpretations of them are as varied as the children themselves, but they are always creative and resourceful. I urge parents of Deaf children to celebrate such knowledge. But perhaps more importantly, I urge them to listen to the Deaf adults of today, for we were once Deaf children. Only those who have been there can "tell it like it is." By forming partnerships, Deaf adults and hearing parents of Deaf children can create a better world for future Deaf children—a world in which no one feels forced to choose between free communication and family ties. With more dialogue between those of us who have been Deaf children and those who love their own Deaf children, we can create a world that values music, dancing, ASL, speech therapy, truth, burning witches, national flags, and yes, even friendly trees.

Christopher Jon Heuer

CHRISTOPHER JON HEUER was born in a small farming community near Neosho, Wisconsin. He received both a B.A. and an M.A. in English from the University of Wisconsin-Milwaukee and is currently working on a Ph.D. in Adult Literacy at George Mason University in Virginia. He is also an English instructor at Gallaudet University in Washington, D.C. He lives in Alexandria, Virginia, with his wife Amy.

The Hands of My Father

Not once did my father sign to me.
He was a farmer; his explanations
were for the ground. Corn, rain,
earth—this was language,
the planting and bringing forth
of things. He did not like talking
to people, their noise and pace
and frantic lives. To him a sense

of hearing was only good for wind
and thunder, for the moaning
of cattle. I remember the hands
of my father, fingers clenched white
like teeth around the steering
wheels of tractors and the grips of
pitchforks; taking refuge from
the movement of my language

among the motions of his life.
Mine was not the kind of silence
that he knew, standing in rows
to be entered like a church—
undisturbed beyond the brush of
the leaves against his face and arms—
in the fields we would not cross
to meet one another.

My kind of silence was flood
and drought. He watched me
as if God had set the locusts on him.
His hands struck the dinner table
with the fast crack of lightning.

My silence was famine and disease,
forces of nature he could not
root out, or control. Or cure.

But now that he is dead, I see
his fingers in the corn, reaching
over the hills and fences to his son,
to say that he is sorry. At the
field's edge, the touch of each
kernel against my palm is a kiss
from his lips. I would go to him
if I knew where to walk.

Bone Bird

You were a bird of bone.
Your wings held everything in
like a rib cage.
You said that deafness
was nothing, and took your
feathers from the dirt.
You blended in like a leaf
to its bed on a forest floor,
brother.

I said deafness was everything,
our blood and our flesh,
the air we breathed and flew in,
the kill in our talons.
I said that deafness was a song
to be spread out in a plume,
painted across the sky
like a rainbow. But to you

deafness was not a song.
With your tongue and your
bone beak and your rib-cage
wings, you blocked out more sky
than a scarecrow in a cornfield.
I painted your name in the air
but you looked away. You were
afraid of the sky, of your own
wings. You held everything in.

Diving Bell

I am alone among familiar faces—
shiny fish that smile at me in hallways
and at dinners, blowing out their lists of
safe questions, sure to be understood. *How
are you*, sprayed out in a fury of white foam.
They wave their great fins so that I will know
it is me they are talking about. My
diving bell is heavy, the oxygen
turns bad fast. Nonetheless I say *I'm fine,*

how are you? Teeth flash and their eyes crinkle,
like happy piranhas. Blowing bubbles.
I laugh with them like I step on the brakes
of my car at red lights. Dull depths, gray streets.
Swimming through one intersection after
another, somewhere else to somewhere else.
On and off, words blinking Morse, or Chinese.
I choke in the bell, I kick myself dead.
The fish watch, and say that I am angry.

But that weight, all that weight. The pressure
builds, creating flying splinters that draw
blood. Going down. I say I am fine. Traffic
flows smooth around me, blinking on and off.
My hands are flat, white, pushing on the glass,
without gesture. There's no air, there's no air!
The fish follow me down in slow spirals,
nervous and a mystery. Somewhere else
to somewhere else. Nothing at all is wrong.

Holiday

She stuffed her guilt
into turkeys, and deep into the
branches of Christmas trees.
This was my mother,
frantic for the next holiday,
her entire life the preparation
for an occasion. Her fingers
were delicate in manipulation
of the crystal dove ornaments
that hung from silver

garlands on our doors and windows.
Her pies rose like angels
with trumpets; her tableware
and china were immaculate.
"See our home," said her home.
Our living room was a cover
from *McCall's*, a defiant testament
of love for her family that radiated
like a flaming Yule log. Paying tribute
was a toast, the undoing of a fine
silk ribbon around a card.

Blow out the candles, eat some
cake! This is my son, the poet-
philosopher! My son speaks "sign
language!" I'm trying to learn! Her
smiles were frosted on like white
icing, her hands whirring noisemakers.

Our conversations were hidden in
containers of New Years sweet
potatoes and hot muffins, dependent
upon holiday formality that

our true feelings would not carry through
a silence broken only by the usual
obligational laughter, around
roasted ducks and polished bottles
of homemade Thanksgiving wine.
Her words were invitations within
gold envelopes, formally reminding
me of dates for dinners that I would not
attend. The writing sounded like an
"I do" at a wedding, which was nothing
more, really, than a cue to weep.

Corresponding Oval

I think that appropriate suicide
methods are one day going to be taught
in kindergarten classrooms.

Tut, tut, children!

Yes!

How many times do we jump?

Once!

And how many times do we cut?

Once!

Which way?

Deep!

———————

Let me tell you about contempt.
When I die I'm going to fuck with
people's corresponding ovals.

I'm going to sugar-coat a gun barrel with cyanide honey; I'll put it in
   my mouth and lick myself
to death. My teeth will shatter around cold blue steel in a deadly rictus
   grin, but I will die
happy simply because there will be no corresponding oval.

How did he die?

( ) Gun   ( ) Poison

_____

Let me tell you about contempt.
I would bleed off balconies yet not jump,
since I can't jump off balconies and not bleed.

I would slice my wrists shallow and yet lean not-very-far over the rail-
     ings. I would
specifically try to hit older women, to splatter the fake white doves on
     their church-going hats
with the red stains of my life. I would try to hit the sports pages of
     briskly-walking middle-
aged men in plaid suit coats, and the blonde-haired Barbie dolls of
     young girls attached by the
hand to their Christmas-gloved mothers.

_____

Let me tell you about *not knowing*.
I think of it and smile.

When I'm dead I want my epitaph to be a grid of Tic-Tac-Toe played
     over and over again on top of itself.
Every oval crossed out by an 'X.' Every space a question. Something
     filled in, yet something
not. Something uncertain, and something uncontained. Something
     asleep,
yet something poised—and watching.

Sometimes it watches me.
And sometimes not.

Listening for the Same Thing

I REMEMBER thinking—just a moment—that my father was dead when I finally found him that night. When it turned out that he wasn't, I wanted to kill him myself.

That was 1985, in the fall. I was fifteen. There was a dance that weekend, so I remember. Dances were a big thing for Jenny and me. We didn't have a normal dating life. At best I was only home every two weeks from the Wisconsin School for the Deaf. If you were in sports it was longer. For the "away" games you got on the bus with the team and drove to some other state to play *their* school for the deaf. Wisconsin played everyone that bordered us, as well as a few states that didn't. Sometimes I wasn't home for a month. The longest I ever stayed away was two.

That was the plan before I met Jenny—to stay as far away from home for as long as possible. Believe me—it wasn't hard, not even with all the fights I was getting into behind the dorms at school. The way I see it, either you pick your battles or they pick you. A high school fight I could win. Against my dad, I couldn't. Simple logic.

It was hard on Jenny though. We tried to compensate for my absences by spending as much time together as possible. She didn't know what she was in for when she said she'd go out with me the summer before. Hell, even I didn't know. I was fourteen at the time. What did I know about dating? I met her at a fireman's picnic because she was working at the soda stand. I had been picking off stones in one of the Johnson's fields—which was the only job you could get in Juneau in the summer if your dad didn't own a factory or a bowling alley or something—right next to town. You could smell the burgers and the brats and the smoke drifting all the way out there, and I was hungry.

When all the farmhands got a break at noon I climbed over the fence and went to get a Pepsi and a hotdog. I thought she was cute as hell, and she was giving *me* the eye too. Jenny said it was the lack of a shirt and the dirty, sweat-streaked farm boy muscles that did it for her. For me, it was her jean cut-offs and the fact that she was from Hustisford, a town about ten miles away—which meant she didn't know about my small-town Juneau reputation as the local deaf dumbshit. It helps if girls don't have that information about you when you're fourteen. We talked a bit after I bought the soda from her. I asked her if she'd still be working that night. She said yes and I went home after work and showered and came back in my best jeans and t-shirt. We ended up making out under the stars in the middle of the football field. That was our first date.

It seemed her high school was always having a dance for something . . . Homecoming, Christmas, Sweetest Day . . . you name it. They had a dress code for everything except Halloween. Jenny really liked all the dressing up, even on the Halloween night when we went as Mark Antony and Cleopatra. And hey, I was a good dancer. Huey Lewis, REO Speedwagon, Journey, Motley Crue—I went out there and I danced to all of it. The music sounded like weird underwater German, but even with my hearing aids off I could still follow the beat. Beyond that there wasn't much to do except grab her during the slow songs and sort of just sway back and forth. I did all right.

There was one bad night with some guys from Juneau, though. Juneau guys knew me from a couple years back. You can imagine what it was like. They would surround me and start chanting "*hey* deaf fucker, what did you *say*, deaf fucker!" while their hands cupped and pulled at their ears. I ended up getting into a fight with this kid that was doing the worst of the hazing. He started walking alongside of us and spat in my ear, so I punched him. Jenny tried to stop it, but by that time I was pumped up. I tackled him and hit everything I could—his face, his nuts, his ribs—before his buddies pulled me off of him. He got up screaming that I fought like a faggot, but he was bleeding worse than I was, and that's all that counts at the end of a fight. Jenny ran and got a teacher from the dance and that was the end of it.

I remember that one night mostly because there was a dance and my dad was late in picking me up to drive me out to Jenny's house.

I didn't have a license. I didn't even have a learner's permit. When it was warm I would bike down to her house, which was about eight miles away by road. In dry weather you could take a shortcut through the marshes that cut the distance in half, but it had rained a lot and everything was under water. Plus it was cold. And plus I was already running a little late. It would take me a half hour at least to get there by bike.

The dance started at seven and I was supposed to be at Jenny's house by six-thirty. I was ready to go by six. I was dressed in my dad's white dress shirt. The collars were pinned down because it was one of those seventies shirts with the disco collars. The shirt went good with my brown chords and brown dress shoes. I wasn't yet sophisticated enough to put on brown socks instead of white socks, but my pants were kind of long and nobody could see my socks anyway.

By six-fifteen he still wasn't home, and that was forty-five minutes later than usual. I kept walking in and out of the house to see if he was coming down the hill. You could see the road best from the front porch. The back door led to our gravel driveway where dad parked the truck. It wasn't easy to see the road from there because the yard light always shined in your eyes. If you went around to the front of the house, the yard light was blocked out and you could watch up the road for headlights.

At six-thirty I went out to check again, but he wasn't there. By the time six forty-five rolled around I was seriously considering walking up there to see if he was even still at the farm. He worked up at the main farm with the big white barn—the one with the Johnson Dairy Farms logo. It was about a mile away.

But I didn't go for two reasons. One, I didn't want to change again, and if I walked up there in my dance stuff I would get it all stinked up. Two, what would happen if I started walking up the hill and he came home from the other direction for some reason? I mean, it wasn't inconceivable—maybe they sent him out to get something in Clyman or Reeseville. He'd arrive home and wonder where the hell I was.

By seven-thirty I was making constant revolving trips out the front and back doors to see if he was either coming down the hill or already parked out front. I wanted to call Jenny but that was always a pain in the ass. We didn't have a TDD back then—we only had a volume dial built into the phone. Even when it was turned up all the way I could barely make out what was being said to me, and it was impossible to discriminate between Jenny's voice and her mother's. Spending a half hour apologizing into a phone that could very well have her mother on the other end wasn't exactly "Plan A" for me, if you take my meaning.

By eight I gave up on the revolving door trips. By nine I just plain gave up. I got undressed and put on sweats and a t-shirt. But I kept glancing out the window just the same, to see if he was coming. And then ten o'clock rolled around.

That was when I decided to go out looking for him. There was no conceivable reason that he should be five and a half hours late getting home. Mostly I was just mad and wanted something to do.

It was cold so I stole my brother's jacket. He had some smokes in one of the pockets. That was a rarity for me. It was hard getting smokes or booze or pretty much anything normal at WSD. You could smoke outside the dorms but only at designated times and even then a pack of cigarettes cost too much to be worth the bother.

I lit up as I walked up the road toward the barn. The cold air and the smoke felt really good as it mixed in my lungs. The coaches could really run the shit out of you during football practices. It was good just to walk and breathe like a normal kid. It was good not to have people slapping your helmet and pushing you to move faster, faster, *faster*! I personally think our head coach would have given *birth* if he had caught me with a cigarette.

I remember thinking about this guy named Jason Bartoletti at school. He had given me a really hard time during my first year at WSD when I didn't know how to sign all that well. I think it really pissed him off that I made the first-string punt return team when I was only a freshman. He was a big guy but I had it all over him in speed. That didn't help much, though, when you had to keep your eye on the ball instead of on him. He used to love slamming into me even after I had waved to signal a fair catch. No matter how many times the coach reamed his ass, he still kept slamming into me with all the force he could get away with. We had a sort of matador thing going . . . he had to slow down enough to be sure he could get me, because I had been side-stepping him lately and it was humiliating to find yourself face down in the dirt while the receiver sprints up the field. But I had to keep one eye on him as well as one eye on the ball, so I had been missing easy catches lately.

The coach had forced us both to run ten laps on the hill earlier last week to punish us for our bullshit. I remembered Jason talking with his buddies in the locker room afterwards. They had a pet name-sign for me . . . it sort of looked like the sign for "crazy" but it was done in front of the forehead instead of near the ear. At WSD it meant "thinks he's hearing." It was the Deaf culture's version of "hey, deaf fucker" reserved for anybody who talked more than signed. Just to piss him off, I'd adopted the name-sign as my own, and even used it in front of the teachers and the coaches.

Jason had used that name-sign and said something about kicking my ass on Sunday when we came back to school. I threw a tape roll at him and flipped him the finger. That was a safe enough move on my part. The coach was in his office at the end of the locker room and if you fought with another player then you got benched. Jason wasn't going to start anything in the locker room. Still, Sunday was tomorrow, and there was the problem of how to get past him and into my room without getting the shit kicked out of me.

Halfway up the hill there was a little inlet that led down into a field. Tractors used it to get down off the road and through the ditch. The inlet was a nice place to stop. It was just beyond the crest of the hill, so you could see the town lights of Juneau along with the stars. If you followed it down a bit you came to a grove of trees that bordered a field. I had a little rock pit set up in there that I used for campfires. If you walked right up to it in the daytime you wouldn't even recognize it because there were a lot of other stones around. We always threw small stones into the grove whenever we were picking off stones during the summertime.

I don't know why I didn't just keep walking toward the barn. I think a part of me knew that he wasn't there. I gathered up some sticks and lit them up with newspaper that I had hidden in a plastic bag under some rocks.

Staring into campfires when it was cold out had a calming effect on me. That, and looking at the stars. I could remember things that way and the memories wouldn't bother me. I started thinking about my dad and our trips to Watertown. He was a good guy when I was a kid, back when we still had the farm. He'd go into town almost every day for something . . . for candy bars and for beer and soda that he liked to drink when he drove the big John Deere tractors out in the fields.

He'd let me jump into the cab of that old, beat-up light blue Ford that we had back then. Sometimes he'd even let me steer—actually *steer* without taking his foot off the gas by so much as an inch. There was never anybody on the roads. Watertown was quiet, and if you lived outside the city limits it was even more quiet.

When we went into town, we had an unspoken agreement. He'd give me a few bucks and I'd go read in the comic book store. He'd go into this bar across the street. I'd have a good hour in the store at least before he'd come to get me. Then we'd drive home, me with a few new comic books and him with a six-pack of Red, White, and Blue.

It was fun back then. He'd let me sit with him on the tractor. Sometimes when it was hot he'd let me drink from his beer bottle—never too much, but enough to get me a bit thick-headed. Sometimes we'd park the tractor in the field near the Rock River. We'd fish down there once in a while if he had some worms around somewhere. I would run up onto the bridge and drop stones into the water. Dad left me alone when the stones were small, but he'd yell at me if they were big ones that I could barely lift. He said I was scaring the fish away. Mostly I just think he didn't want me to drop one of those things on my foot.

I remembered how things changed once we lost the farm. It went under because of debt, but that wasn't his fault. A lot of farms went under in the late seventies—especially in Dodge County. After we lost it the new owners let him work on it for a while. We even got to live in our house—paying rent on it instead of paying off the mortgage. When we went into town, he'd pass me a whole five-dollar bill and send me across the street. He stayed in the bar longer, too. I'd get comics and then a malt at the restaurant up the street. After a while he didn't come looking for me. I always had to go to the bar to get him.

We had a new thing going by the time we moved to Juneau a few months later. He'd take me into town and the six-pack became a twelve-pack, and then a case. The five became a ten, then a twenty every week by the time I became thirteen. I think he was paying for his words. He didn't say much of anything after a while and I think he felt guilty about it somewhere in there. I think he knew that he should be saying something throughout the days and years, and that the silence in our new house was the result of some kind of debt he wasn't paying or something. So he started paying with his twenties. By then he'd paid so much debt in so many different forms and shapes and sizes that he didn't even question the act of pulling out his wallet anymore. He just felt he owed somebody and handed his money over.

I never did go to the barn. When the fire burned out I started walking home again. As I approached the driveway I could see our back yard. From the dim purple circle of illumination under the yard light I could see the outline of a car parked at the far corner of our back yard.

I broke into a light jog. Was someone visiting? Why did he park so far down there like that? When I got home I ran right into the house to see if someone was waiting inside. I had the weird feeling that my dad would be home sleeping or something and that I should wake him up to tell him that someone wanted to talk to him.

But dad wasn't on the couch. There was nobody home, not my mom and not my brother. It was eleven o'clock at night.

I went outside again and walked down toward the car. The back lawn was about fifty yards long. That's common in Wisconsin, where a lot of people live out in the country. Some people have entire forests bordering their yards. We had a couple of trees. As I got closer I could see that the car wasn't so much *parked* as it was slightly *crashed into* one of the corner trees.

The damage was light, as far as I could see. I circled around it and saw it was my dad's car. There was just a bent fender. You would never miss it on that heap. I couldn't see my dad, though. I wondered where the hell he was.

Then I saw him. He was lying on his side passed out on the front seat. I could just barely make him out and had to use my lighter to see him better. In the glow of the flame I saw about four or five beer cans on the floor. There was also an open twelve-pack of Red, White, and Blue sitting on the back seat.

I saw that the gear shift was in neutral and that told me the full story. He was always forgetting to set the car in park. . . .

The same thing had happened in the spring before that. Jenny had been over to my house that night. We'd only been dating for about eight months at that time. Her dad was real good about letting her come over. He knew that we wanted to spend as much time together as possible. We'd go upstairs and watch movies in my room. There were no captions on the little television set that I had up there and Jenny would try her best to sign what was going on in the movies. I liked watching her move in the glow of the television behind her. I once told her it helped me to see through her shirt. She would smile and fool around and do a little strip tease once in a while.

We had come back from a dance and then fallen asleep on my bed while watching television. I only woke up at eleven forty-five. She had curfew at midnight.

"*Shit*. Jenny, get up." I pulled the chair away from the door and went downstairs while she got dressed.

My dad was passed out on the couch. There were three or four beer cans on the floor next to him. I gently nudged them under the couch with my toe as I shook his shoulder.

"*Dad. Hey, pop.*" I started out whispering but realized stupidly that this would only keep him from waking up. "*Dad!* Hey. Come on." I shook his shoulder a few times.

When he's really bad his eyes won't roll down from up in his skull. You've got to slap him a few times and wiggle his jaw. It's the only thing that brings him around. If his eyes aren't down from his skull then he's not awake, and I shit you not when I tell you that I've seen him have entire phone conversations with people when his eyes were rolled up like that. He would never remember what he had said when he came to a few hours later. It became so bad eventually that he would wake up with the phone in his hand and rip the whole thing out of the wall because he couldn't remember.

Finally his eyes rolled down. So did his eyebrows. He seemed to get mad whenever he saw me.

"*What?*" he growled.

"Pop. We gotta go. We're late getting Jenny home."

"Yeah, yeah." This was his traditional response. It meant a head nod and an average of four more hours of sleep.

I shook him again. "Dad!"

This brought him out of it. "*Yeah!*" he barked, slapped my hand away and sat up. Then he rubbed his eyes with his fingers. "Just wait a goddamned minute!"

Jenny had followed me down by this time. She was waiting in the dining room.

"Pop. Jenny's here. She's waiting. We gotta take her home."

He looked at me blearily and sighed. I knew he'd be okay when he got up and started heading towards the bathroom. I put my arm around Jenny's shoulders and turned her around so she wouldn't see him. He was still in his underwear.

"Come on," I told her. "Let's go wait in the car."

I took her out and we climbed into the back seat. It was cold, even in the late spring. Colder even than the early fall. Wisconsin was always cold.

She shivered in her jacket. "Is he coming?" she signed. I guess she spoke, too. Her lips moved. But it was hard to see them in the dark. It was hard to see her signs, too.

"Yeah," I answered.

"Is he drunk?"

That surprised me. She usually wasn't so blunt like that.

"Nah. He's okay."

She didn't look convinced. I grabbed her hands and blew on them to keep them warm. I told her I loved her and she smiled and kissed me. It seemed I was saying it more and more often just to take her mind off things and not because I just felt like saying it.

The back door opened. Dad came out still in his underwear. He pulled out his dick and started pissing on the back lawn. I laughed for some strange reason. He had just been in the bathroom and now he was pissing again and he was in his underwear in front of my girlfriend. That just struck me as funny. I laughed.

Jenny punched me in the shoulder and signed for me to shut up. My dad stuck his dick back in his underwear and went inside. Sometimes he didn't finish peeing when he did that. His underwear was always yellow and stained.

I rubbed my shoulder. "What the fuck are you punching *me* for?" I asked.

"Is he *drunk?*" She was really mad. I was surprised.

"What? No. No. He'll be all right in a second."

"Dan! *Bullshit!* He's drunk!"

"Hey. Jenny. Calm down." I tried to put my arms around her. She pushed me away.

"Don't touch me."

"What you mad at *me* for?"

"You're going to let him drive us while he's drunk."

There was a game that we played. Well, it was a game that I played with her. It was called the Eyebrow Game. My dad was a master at it. At the dinner table, for example—if my mom tried to say something banal, like if she said that she wanted to paint the living room or something, he'd take this long pause from eating. Man, it seemed like a glacier could creep across America before that pause was over, you know? And then he'd just raise his right eyebrow. It was like a baseball bat going up over all of our heads. Mom would never say anything banal after that.

I played the game with Jenny. "Come on," I said, letting my eyebrows lift. "He's not *drunk*. He's like that all the time. He's just tired."

"Crap. He can barely stand."

I stared at her and kept my eyebrows up.

"He's drunk, Dan. I'm not letting him drive us."

I didn't answer.

"Dan," she said.

I kept looking at her. Finally she was silent.

I didn't know what to do. She looked really scared. I saw that the keys were still in the ignition. It only took me a few seconds to calculate the odds of whether or not he had walked back inside and just fallen asleep again. They were pretty good.

"Okay, fine," I said. "I'll drive."

Jenny started to cry.

"Come on," I said. "Knock it off. It's him or me, right?"

She put her fingers to her eyes.

"Hey, *you're* the one bitching about who's in shape to drive where," I said. "You don't want him to drive? Fine. I'll drive."

"Let me call my father, Dan," she signed.

"No. I'm driving." I moved to push the back door open.

She grabbed my jacket. "Dan! You don't even have a license!"

I shrugged her away. "I can drive a tractor—I can drive this."

"No!" Her hands were defiant.

I pushed her away again and started to get out of the car. Then I saw the back door of the house open. It was my dad. He had his pants on and was walking toward us.

When he got in the car he spent five minutes patting through his pockets for his keys until I told him that they were still in the ignition. He almost went off the road three times on the way to Jenny's place. When we pulled into her driveway she ran from the car without closing the door.

I remember being pissed off at him. I didn't get out of the car and come around front. I just pulled the back door closed and said "drive." He almost went off the road three times on the way home, too. When he finally pulled into our driveway he left the car in neutral instead of park. He didn't even know that the engine was still running when he got out. He was too drunk to notice.

"Pop. You son of a *bitch*." I could smell the beer drifting up out of the car as I stood next to him. What time was it? Midnight? Eleven-thirty? Mom would be home soon. I had to get him out of there. I had to get the car off the lawn.

He was heavy. I had to plant my feet just to pull him upright by his jacket. His eyes were rolled way back into his head and they wouldn't roll back down no matter how hard I shook him.

"Dad? Come on . . . *fuck* . . ." No choice now. I leaned down and pulled his feet out of the car by his pants cuffs. Once they were planted on the ground I grabbed his jacket again and pulled.

I learned the trick from Mom. She walked him to bed all the time before he started sleeping on the couch on a permanent basis. You stand next to him, you hook your hands in his belt, and you walk him. An alcoholic never quite passes out, as I've said. You can get him to do all kinds of things in his sleep.

"Come on, Dad. *Walk.*" He walked. He would have staggered had I not been holding onto him, but with my guidance we made slow, shuffling angles toward the back door of the house. He was leaning heavily on me. I had to balance him with my arm and leg while I reached out to pull the door open.

There was an explosion of hot wetness down my leg. His pants were dark and wet where he had urinated on himself. It had seeped right through my sweatpants.

I closed my eyes in disgust and pulled the door open. Then I had to balance him again to pull it shut again. No sooner than I had twisted around did I feel something hot splattering against my legs.

"*Jesus Christ*, dad . . ." but he wasn't pissing again. He had his hands on his knees and he was puking all over the place. I held his collar while he heaved and gasped. Finally he puked himself out, at least for the time being.

I dragged him to the couch and let him fall down. And then came the Ritual.

First the car. Start it, put it in reverse, and back it up to the driveway. Throw the young willow sapling that my brother had been tending all summer into the ditch, because it had been severed when the car ran it over.

Then the sidewalk. I hosed it down, cleaning off the piss. Thank God the outside spigot was right there. Very strategic. I dragged the hose into the entryway and sprayed out as much of the puke as I could. There was a broom in there. I used that and Dawn dishwashing soap to get rid of the smell on the floor. Finally I washed off the hose itself.

Next came *him*. Pull his shirt off over his head. Untie the shoes and yank them off, then yank down his pants around his hips. His underwear was stained and yellow. I threw a blanket over him and put on my mom's rubber dishwashing gloves before I pulled those off. The whole mess went into a laundry basket along with my dirty stuff. I took the clothes down to the laundry room naked and dumped them in the wash with two cups of soap.

Then *me*. A long, hot shower, using shampoo to scrub the filth and the stench off my legs. With a towel wrapped around me I went upstairs and got fresh sweats, a t-shirt, and socks.

And finally him. I kept the blanket over him and the dishwashing gloves on while I put a little Dawn soap on a rag and wiped the piss off his legs and the mess off of his mouth. The whole thing made me gag but I kept going and I got it done. Then I threw the rag in the wash with the rest of the clothes and washed my hands one more time. I realized I had forgotten to put a bucket next to him by the couch and ran to get one. He hardly ever puked a second time, but you could never be too careful.

My mom came home at around twelve-thirty. She saw me sitting in the chair watching the muted yet crackling character of Hawkeye Pierce prance around through that green army tent Swamp-thing that he lived in. She looked at my naked father lying on the couch, covered in a blanket with a bucket at his side.

"Did you go to your dance?" she said. Not signed . . . *said*. And I understood her perfectly well, too. I didn't have to lipread her, I didn't even have to look up. I simply knew exactly what it was that she was going to say. It was the only thing that she *could* have said, the only thing that would have made everything seem normal again. The illusion of normalcy was all that mattered. I had played my part by cleaning up—she played hers by telling him to get up and leading him into the bedroom.

After a while I got up too. Normally I would have gone upstairs before she got home. But I wanted her to see. I wasn't sure why.

The next day there was a twenty dollar bill on the table. Mom said she'd drive me to the Greyhound bus depot. Usually Jenny's mom or dad drove me so that she could wait with me until the bus came to take me back to WSD. But it was Sunday and Jenny hadn't called. Or if she had, my mom wasn't telling me about it. So I figured she was mad that I didn't show up the night before.

My dad came in unexpectedly just then. He usually wasn't around during the afternoons. We had one of our long pauses. The money sat on the table between us.

"That's yours," he said, pointing.

I looked at it . . . then back at him.

"Take it. You'll need some money for the week."

I made no move to pick it up. I stared at him until my eyes began to water. My hands clenched into fists. It was the first time in my life that I had ever dared defy my father for even a few moments.

He erupted all at once—suddenly and furiously—and rushed at me, knocking the chair over as he grabbed the money off the table. "*Take the fucking money, Dan!*" he shouted, and stuffed it down my shirt. I made no move to stop him, and I made no move to help him. He was back out the door in three seconds flat. It was over that quickly.

My mom finally broke the long silence that followed.

"You should take the money, Daniel," she said. "You need that money for school." She sounded so normal. It was frightening to watch her.

What can I say? I took the money. It was expected, wasn't it? It's what I was being paid to do in the first place.

I got past Jason that night, by the way. I got off the bus and just went to my floor to get Mark. Mark was one of the dormitory counselors. We had a good deal going . . . he always helped me make phone calls and I kept my ass out of as much trouble as I could. I think he had dozens of such private agreements among the football players. If not for that we would be getting into shit all the time when the coach gave us passes on the weekends to go into town.

I dialed Jenny's number and Mark made sure she was on the line. Then I spent the next half an hour apologizing into a silent phone. She could have hung up at any time and I wouldn't have known. There was no volume control on that line—there was only a TDD, and Jenny didn't have a TDD. I said I was sorry and that I loved her and then I hung up. I'd have to wait a few days for a letter from her in order to get her reply.

The fight with Jason didn't happen until Thursday, and it happened mostly because I had been waiting for that letter and it didn't come when mail call finally rolled around that afternoon. I spent the whole practice in a grim state of focus. Jason missed me every time on the punt returns. I made him look like shit. The coach ran him up the hill for five laps every time he missed me. He was pretty pissed in the locker room, and he was still pissed at supper.

I surprised myself by picking a fight with him.

"Come on out to the locker room, fucker," I said, and pushed his milk carton onto his lap. I started walking towards the door before he could react. Neither of us wanted to start a fight in front of the counselors. But after dinner you had an hour of free time. Nobody would be looking for us outside.

I ran to the locker room ahead of him and grabbed my helmet off its hook. When he came through the door I bashed it over his face. When he bent down and grabbed his nose, I bashed it over the back of his skull. He went down and I kicked him in the nuts and in the eye. I knelt on his solar plexus and grabbed his throat, squeezing. He was in no shape to push me off. At any other time, it wouldn't have been much of a contest, but I got him good. He didn't put up any kind of a fight at all.

I dug my knee into his sternum and grabbed his jaw. I pointed and shoved my finger into his forehead. "You," I signed. "Leave me alone or I'll kill you." Then I got off him. I knew he wouldn't tell the coach or the counselors. We kept things to ourselves in that school.

When I got back to the dorms one of the counselors came up and handed me a letter from Jenny. He said it got sent to the wrong floor by mistake. He looked at my face and asked me why I was so red. I told him I'd been out running laps.

Jenny and I stayed together for about a year after that. When we finally broke up, it was because of an accumulation of everything. She couldn't take it anymore—all the fighting and all the stuff with my dad. I was hurt but not really surprised.

I remember our last phone call. Mark helped me make the call. I told him that I needed him to do a two-way interpreting thing this time, as opposed to just getting her on the line and letting me talk. He was okay with that. He was always distant from things because he wanted it to be your phone call and not his. You got the sense that he was listening without listening. I could sort of phase him right out of the situation and actually believe that it was just me on the phone with her alone.

I called Jenny to see if she wanted to get together that coming weekend as friends. It would be the first weekend home that I would have to face without her in nearly two years. I needed her to help me get through it. I asked her if she'd please get together with me and I couldn't stop my voice from breaking. Mark put his hand on my shoulder and spoke to her for a while and then hung up the phone.

"She can't Dan," he signed. "She said she can't handle the feelings right now. She hopes you'll understand that."

Mark had been a sergeant in Vietnam. His wife left him and he'd been a drunk for almost ten years. I told him about my dad and he told me about getting sober in A.A. I told him about taking my dad's clothes off so I could wash them. He told me about what it was like when he came back from 'Nam. Out of the jungles and into the streets. He screamed once because he saw some chick eating a pink ice cream cone. He talked about not being able to connect to reality, about feeling like you were living in somebody else's body. Mark understood things and I understood Mark. I appreciated his being there and helping me through that call.

"Yeah," I said, and nodded. "Okay." He put his hand on my shoulder and rubbed my neck. I tried like hell to keep from breaking. I didn't even come close.

That weekend I went home. My mom picked me up, which was strange for me. Usually it was Jenny and her mom, or just Jenny alone after she got her license.

I went right up to my room and shut the door. Mom left me alone. I figured she thought I'd come down when I got hungry.

But in fact I just went to sleep. I slept until three in the morning. I only woke up because I had to go to the bathroom, but I didn't go. Instead I just lay there staring at the ceiling. After a while I started to cry.

I thought I was being quiet, but I guess I wasn't. In the darkness my bedroom door opened. The only illumination in the room was from the neighbor's yard light across the road. I couldn't tell who it was right away—at first I thought it was my mom. But it turned out to be my dad.

I didn't move when he sat down next to me. My tears were hot and stinging in the corners of my eyes. I made no attempt to wipe them away.

He did it for me. He used the back of his hand and dried my cheeks. He ran his fingers quickly through my hair and awkwardly patted my head.

"Move over," I think he said. In any case he pushed me gently across the mattress. Then he lay down next to me with his head at my feet. He crossed his arms over his chest and probably closed his eyes. Or maybe he stared up at the ceiling. I don't know. It was too dark to tell. All I know is that I studied his face, and the harder I looked at him, the more it seemed like his eyes were closed. After a while I thought that was a pretty good idea and closed my own eyes. When I awoke in the morning he was gone.

I stayed in my room all day, even after my mom came up and told me to come down and eat. I only went down to go to the bathroom, and after that I only went down when everyone was asleep later on that night. Dad had already put out a twenty-dollar bill on the table for me. I went into the kitchen and made a sandwich. When I came back out he was standing in the dining room watching me.

"Are you okay?" he asked. All around him was a silence that drowned out his words. It was strange. I couldn't understand what he was talking about.

I'll tell you something about deafness. When you're deaf, you learn to get through your life by watching either for words or the silence—you listen with your eyes. After a while you realize that words and silence are the exact same thing. They're interchangeable. You can't have one without the other. Something has to break the silence, and something has to break the words. You listen for the same thing and you find that you understand everything important. You understand a hell of a lot more than most people think you do.

But that night was strange. I listened to his words, I listened to his silence. For the first time in my life they weren't telling me the same thing.

"That money's yours," he said, gesturing. I refused to look at it. I refused to look down—I refused to look away. I think we both realized at the same time that I wouldn't be taking it. He'd have to break my neck if he wanted to shove it down my shirt again. I wasn't angry and I didn't hate him. But he'd have to break my neck.

He seemed lost. In a way I could almost understand. Money is solid—not just a physical object but also an action. Pass over a twenty and you've done something concrete. You can measure it . . . something paid and something owed. Everything else was awkward and confusing and uncertain and full of risk because you couldn't measure what you were giving.

When I didn't take the money he went back into the living room to lie down on the couch. Our eyes met for one brief moment and in that moment the silence suddenly made sense to me again. It spoke and told me exactly what his words would have said, had he chosen to speak.

I have no control, is what he said.

No, I agreed. *You don't.*

It was the first mutual understanding that we ever reached.

Carmen Cristiu

CARMEN CRISTIU was born on September 15, 1962, in Bucharest, Romania. She attended primary, elementary, and high schools for hearing pupils. She is a graduate of the Planning and Economic Cybernetics Department of the Economical Studies Academy. At the present time, she works as a programming analyst for the National Society of Telecomunications, ROMTELECOM S.A. She is also vice-president for cultural affairs in the Bucharest branch of the National Association of the Deaf of Romania. Cristiu has participated in and received awards at many cultural contests. She got very good results at all of the "Creative Literary Contests" (Mamaia 1996, Botosani 1997, Herculane Bads 1999). She won first place in the prose/fiction category. She is currently working on a history of the deaf association in Romania and is a staff writer at the newspaper, *The Voice of Silence*, where she writes articles on different topics, especially cultural reports and the regular column, "Reconstitutions." She is very passionate about deaf history.

Leaves on the Water

Sorrow swooped upon our love,
Which crawled into a floe
That would not melt
So it protected an undying fire
That would not burn out.
But for the two of us to live on,
Something had to die.

Which of the two got to die?
We didn't know.
Neither did the old rivers
That we strewed with dead leaves . . .

Is It A Sin?

I wasn't born from sin,
But from a much stronger love.
An old love, of two people
Who suddenly were lost.
Life, in its strange ways,
Brought them together again,
When they were gold
And have spent a lifetime
Raising other people's children.

Those other people's children
Raised out of too much love,
Like me,
Born from a much too stronger love,
Today and forever more
Are bringing up my children,
Born from sin,
But beholders of the strong love
From the begging . . .

My Mother

One night, when stars were dancing,
Without me ever hearing them,
Mother taught me the magical song
Of the Lucifer,
Holding me tight against her bosom
So that the pain and fever,
Which, since then, have never returned,
Would go away.
I was lost in the Lucifer's dance,
Who, like me,
Couldn't hear.

Gaynor Young

GAYNOR YOUNG was born in Nakuru, Kenya, in 1961, but she has spent most of her life in South Africa. She became deaf as a result of a severe fall, which also resulted in other physical and mental injuries, while performing in *Camelot* in 1989. She has turned the tragedy around and has used it as the basis for her writing and for her continued success as an actress. She has written a book, *My Plunge to Fame*, and developed her own one-woman show.

My Plunge to Fame

now the ears of my ears awake and
now the eyes of my eyes are opened

E E CUMMINGS, "[i thank You God for most this amazing]"

WHY READ *My Plunge to Fame?* Of what interest will the book be to the deaf community? Of what interest will the book be to the community as a whole? I would love to say this book should be read because the writing is on a par with Gabriel Garcia Marquez, James Joyce, and William Shakespeare. But unfortunately I would be lying.

However, I have probably lived a life as interesting as the lives of those esteemed authors and perhaps a more unusual one. This story is about that life.

My life.

Christopher Reeve wrote his autobiography *Still Me* and disabled people have read it and loved it. But it also has an attraction for people who are not disabled in any way. It is a book about a human being. It is brave, funny, and deeply moving. In the same way *My Plunge to Fame* is about Gaynor Young, who was an actress and is now deaf, spastic, and brain damaged but who has not lost her sense of humor nor her love for humanity. I hope my book is as funny, insightful and above all, as inspiring as Christopher Reeve's autobiography. It is certainly as honest.

I WAS THE understudy for the part of Guinevere in the musical *Camelot*. On the ninth of December in 1989 I was called upon to take over the role. Which I did—brilliantly! The scene preceding the interval I was meant to exit and change into this beautiful robe and then come back onstage. Somehow I missed my footing and fell eighteen meters (five-story drop) into an unguarded elevator shaft. I broke both arms and legs. I broke four ribs. I broke every single bone in my face. If you can picture an egg dropping onto the floor, that was my skull! It took the doctors and all of the king's horses and all the king's men a six-hour operation to get me together again.

I was in a deep coma for three and a half weeks and a semi-coma for the following three weeks. I had 40 percent of my eyesight. I was spastic on the right side of my body. I could not walk. I could not talk.

And I was deaf!

Four years later I was back on stage performing in my own one-woman show, which I had written myself. And here I am now—a published author!

My book tells of my life before the accident and the journey I have traveled since—the ups, the downs, the triumphs, and the deep depressions.

My DRIVING force just after my accident was to act again; to get back onstage. Acting, for me, was what I used to do in my old life. Acting was normal. How I longed to be normal once again.

My friends went off to auditions, rehearsals, and performances. I went off to physiotherapy, occupational therapy, speech therapy, and psychotherapy. Very different.

About three years after my accident, my psychotherapist finally got me to accept that the Gaynor Young that had played the part of Guinevere in *Camelot* on December 9, 1989, had been killed. She had died that day.

And yet, *I* am alive! With this I comes the deafness, blindness, and spasticity. It was from this point, that I began the wonderful journey of acceptance; the acceptance of the "new" Gaynor.

When I went deaf I was horrified and, yes, deeply ashamed. Three months before my accident I was at a cocktail party and a deaf man was pointed out to me. I then made sure that I was always at opposite ends of the room from him, that we never made contact except to smile at each other in passing. I deeply regretted doing so because he was a complete dish. But I didn't know how to handle him; how loud I must S-H-O-U-T; or what I would do if he were unable to hear me. I didn't know sign language, either, so I avoided him at all costs.

Then, suddenly, I was deaf. Bad enough that I couldn't hear but to be labeled "deaf" was too horrendous for words. I mean, deaf people weren't normal. They were . . . well, yes . . . deaf! So I grew my hair long in order to hide that dreadful tell-tale hearing aid. And there was no way that I would ever let on to a soul that I could not hear them, that I had perhaps missed what they were saying.

"Really!" became the word that I used in all situations where I did not have a clue as to what was going on.

"What do you think of Mbeki, our new Prime minister?"

Hearty laugh, "Really!"

I was a sad case.

Then I discovered the Durban Deaf Club. I arrived for the first of my sign language lessons full of hope that at last I would be able to communicate with other deaf people. But, sadly, I was never to master sign language. My major problem was my eyesight. My eyes find it impossible to watch two hands at the same time. Also, the speed with which the hands move is very difficult for me to follow. Being spastic on my right side increased my difficulty. I studied sign language for four months and then gave it up.

But those were four of the most important months of my life. They showed me that deaf people were the same as others, the only difference being that they could not hear. People whose eyesight is not good wear glasses. People whose hearing is not good wear hearing aids.

Since I have been deaf I have learned to listen. Not only with the little hearing I have left, but also with my sight, my touch, and my smell. People speak in different ways and mean different things; one learns what to look for and what to sense. That was just one of the things that I learned at the Deaf Club.

In 1994 Maralin Vanrenen, a director, contacted me with a proposal that took my breath away. She wanted to direct me in a performance. Not me acting as a character but rather as Gaynor Young telling her story.

"But I don't know what to say. There isn't enough that's interesting in my life," I said.

"You have got one of the most interesting lives I know. Don't be pathetic. Sit at your computer and write your script. Then e-mail it to me. You have got two months. We open in April."

And so I sat down in front of my computer and began to write.

In March I went up to Johannesburg and rehearsals with Maralin began. We opened on April 12 to standing ovations. I had acted for seven years and never, ever had I evoked such a response from the audience. They laughed and they cried. I performed in Johannesburg, Durban, Cape Town, and a return season in Johannesburg. The audience loved me. As a result I began to discover a love of myself returning.

One evening after the performance, I heard a knock on my dressing room door. "Come in," I shouted.

"I won't take up much of your time," this man said. "Last night I came and saw your show. I brought a friend with me who two weeks previously had been let out of the mental home that she had been staying in. When she was eleven years old she was raped repeatedly by her father. After your show we were walking across the foyer when all of a sudden she stopped. She faced me and said, "Okay. Okay, now I shall begin to fight.""

How could my show have that kind of influence on a person?

I could understand it having an effect on disabled people. Sure. Okay. But "normal," everyday, run-of-the-mill people? And yet it did. Afterwards, in the bar, I chatted with people and I found that they regarded me as an "inspiration." Me! An inspiration! That totally blew my mind.

I DECIDED to write a book about myself. Initially my editor, Shirley Johnston, and I had a major disagreement. She wanted me to write my autobiography and I wanted my book to be composed mainly of essays about the various things that were important to me—my deafness, my acceptance of the way I am, etc.

"My accident has impaired my memory. How can I write my autobiography when I can barely remember anything of my past?"

"*You* might not, but other people do. They will fill you in," encouraged Shirley.

My editor is a person equally as stubborn as I and in this case, in retrospect, I am glad to say she got her own way. I e-mailed, faxed, wrote letters, and spoke to my friends and family and gradually I began to fill in the previously blank spaces of nothingness in my life.

Shirley is a friend who I have known for the past fifteen years. Whenever I concluded a chapter I would e-mail it to her, and she would read it and then comment accordingly. When I sent her the chapter on my professional years in the theater, I included the statement, "I spent seven years acting professionally and what blissful years these were."

"Utter garbage!" Shirley wrote to me. "You were frustrated, ecstatic, angry, filled with joy, depressed, nervous, confident . . . be truthful."

"But if I'm truthful, the reader will hate me," I wailed.

"If you're truthful, the reader will identify with you and relate to you."

And so, with great trepidation, I wrote as honestly as I could, brutally so at times. Now, when I speak to readers of my book, my truthfulness seems to be one of the book's major drawing cards.

Despite my brain damage, my impaired sight, my spastic hand, my defective memory, I managed to finish my book. I never thought it would be read by anyone other than friends and family, but it is being used in school classes and it has been nominated for a major award.

I am proud of my book.

John Lee Clark

JOHN LEE CLARK is the founder and EdiCurator of *The Tactile Mind*, a literary magazine of the signing community and its Press. He is an alumnus of the Minnesota State Academy for the Deaf and Gallaudet University and is now studying at the University of Minnesota. He is also the recipient of the Optimist Club International Grand Prize in Oratory and the Robert F. Panara Award for Poetry, among other awards. Clark lives in the Twin Cities with his wife, Adrean, and their son, Jael Ethas.

Q

Auburn is her chignon
And yirring for cowslip's
Chamomile husbandry.
Compare but once:
~ Her bottom's fresh
        palm-toasted buns;
~ Spoor of calyptra-paven
                    congress.

I, a disarmed connoisseur
Of her pretty hips and thighs
            (that is, phat)
and *lightly of her classified
            coccyx,
Cannot luxate my lunt
From the touchwood of her
                    crenelated
toenail.

"No, you cannot
            kiss
the beautiful welt.
You created it, yes;
it is your copyright;
but as long as the pain
remains . . ."

Her *lashing performance
Cannot be recaptured
By encystment
                in the bluest
            snafu of glinting ice

Nor by detonation, no;
But in the marly swale of
An absurd poet's memory.

* s: in another slightly slashing
poem you'll imagine but not read.

Exuberance

The great blue whale is flowing
Smooth as Reykjavikian chocolate
When deep in the hyaline gloam—
Glade of cyaneous chimaeras
Who, at least, can skim
Her ponderous burden

And her pyriform respiration
(even though the sprays are reputed
to be syntheses of concealment);
Cryeth she, the great blue whale: Soft
(which is, we feel, no more
than a lark, being acephalous

and rewoven by lissome
dolphins stippled gray
in a milkshake gradation
of porphyry if it could be
pared and palliated
into a cappuccino incarnation)

Exu
Ber
Ance
Exuberance, exuberance,
Exuberance that shames
By daubing this opus:

Babel of aqueous antlers
Zona pellucida-imbued tassels
Unbraiding, melting skyward,
Lustrous and shining—
Dissolving into millions of prisms . . .
Each one a cameolet of aurora light.

Carl Wayne Denney

Born in Indiana, Carl Wayne Denney was deafened by spinal meningitis at six years of age. He graduated from the Kentucky School for the Deaf in 1985 and from Gallaudet University in 2000. During his student years he founded the short-lived *Gallaudetian* and twice won the MacDougall creative writing contest. He went on to be the sports editor for *Deaf Nation* and has been a columnist for *Silent News* since 2000.

Denney is currently the Assistant Dean of Students at the New Mexico School for the Deaf in Santa Fe. He and his wife, Tuesday, have three sons. In his spare time, he enjoys boxing and playing basketball. He also coaches a small basketball club in Santa Fe and serves on the executive board of the United States of America Deaf Basketball, Inc.

Borrowed Time

IT WAS IN Blowing Rock that Carl told Lynn how tired he was of all this driving back and forth, from his job in Kentucky to her home in North Carolina. It had been a year now that he'd been doing that, and he was bone-dead-tired of it, period.

"Time I settled around here, don't you think?" he said, when she came out of Van Heusten's. It was near Christmas time, and it was snowing, although there wasn't much snow on the ground yet.

"What do you mean?" she asked, not really noticing the set look on his face. She rarely did at times like this, when he made a decision.

"My moving out here, silly," he said, taking the packages she thrust out. He wrapped the plastic handles around his hands, and walked after her. She had taken a few steps forward, already thinking of the next item to hunt up. She wanted everyone she knew to have a Christmas present.

"I'm going into Belk's, honey. You want to come in this time?" she asked, already heading in the direction of the entrance. He shook his head and said, "I think I'll wait out here again. I got a lot of thinking to do."

"Well, don't think so much," she said, with a small smile as she went into Belk's. The store was already full, and she hoped she'd get what she came looking for, whatever it was.

Carl sat on one of the benches lining the walk and watched the people walking by, all chipper and merry. He wondered if they realized that they were lucky, far luckier than he was.

Or so he thought, sitting there, waiting for his girlfriend to come out with yet more bundles for him to carry around. The jeep wasn't far off, and maybe he should just go and drop those off.

So he got up and went around the bench, leaving her in the store. There wasn't much traffic, despite the volume in the stores, and he looked both ways before he crossed the road. The jeep was ahead.

The Expedition came out of nowhere and hit the brakes in front of him, sliding on a wet spot. He stood where he was, watching it slide his way. He was right in front of it, and despite the impending collision, he felt no fear.

It slid closer, and he could see the driver's look of apprehension through the windshield. He had that look of "Now I'm fucked. Why doesn't he move?" as Carl stood there, unmoving.

"Do I look like a frozen rabbit?" he wondered as the Expedition finally stopped, two feet from him. He gave a wan smile, and walked off. He knew the driver was still inside breathing a sigh of relief, and perhaps cursing a little. He also knew that in five minutes, he'd be forgotten.

He dimly wondered if he should tell Lynn, as the adrenaline was already fading, the experience becoming a memory.

So he dropped the packages off in the back of the jeep, slamming it shut with a firm hand, feeling its resounding thud. He looked into the gray sky and watched the snowflakes fall upon his face, coming from nowhere, yet from above, where there was only darkness.

He closed his eyes. There was only silence, with the occasional snowflake settling on his face, chilling him a little with its wetness as it melted. He imagined himself naked and soaring in the sky, a warm breeze blowing gently upon his body and his wet hair, for no particular reason.

He opened his eyes, and everything was the same, still. So he walked back in the direction of Belk's, where the bench was, where Lynn would find him waiting.

THE DRIVE home was slow, with heavy traffic and the snow making everybody a little more careful than usual, as if the winding drive down from the mountain village wasn't enough by itself. Carl drove, and Lynn reached over to place her left hand on his right leg occasionally, rubbing it in a show of love and affection. Carl welcomed it immensely.

ARE WE ALL amoebas, floating around the planet, nothing ever real, or lasting, with only history books to tell us that events and people and things actually occurred? Are we all just flesh and blood, walking flesh and blood, blood held in flesh, and flesh with bones in it, and were we just there one moment, gone the next, leaving behind nothing but an empty apartment of books, basketball trophies, and a television blaring static?

Empty clothes, which once a warm, breathing amoeba filled out and wore?

These were his thoughts as they drove home, and when they arrived, they found that Lorraine, Lynn's mother, had left a message on the answering machine. On it, she said she'd be staying in St. Augustine another week because she and Stan were enjoying it more than they thought they would.

"They're fucking like rabbits," Carl told Lynn with a sly grin.

She smiled, punching him lightly in the arm.

Later that night, after a supper of spaghetti and garlic bread with chilled cokes and a dessert of cheesecake, they cuddled up on the couch to watch a video. The video was called *Heavy*.

"It's not about you, is it?" Lynn teased. Carl made a face.

"I'm not that fat!" he said, rubbing his belly.

She grabbed a little flab on her second try. "You're on your way, the way you've been gobbling everything this week," she said.

"Took you a couple times to get some fat off me; besides, you cook too good," he said, laughing.

"I love you," she said, looking into his eyes. He looked right back.

"I love you, too."

He started the movie, and she cried at the end.

"YOU ALWAYS get movies that make me cry," she said after he came back from taking the empty glasses and plates back into the kitchen.

"You didn't cry at *Scream* or *Metro*."

"They weren't real movies."

He gave a look of deep thought, "What were they then?"

"Make-a-buck movies!" she said.

"At least, they made a couple million dollars."

"Still, they weren't real movies," she insisted.

"What's a 'real' movie?' he asked.

"*The Remains of the Day, The Age of Innocence,* and *The English Patient,* to name a few."

"I cried at *The English Patient.* That was a real movie, I agree," he said. That movie had power. Graceful and utterly beautiful.

"I'm glad you recommended it," she said, opening the blankets she had wrapped around herself. "Come on in; let's watch Jerry Springer. He should be on right now."

"Is that real?" he laughed as he got in, and they cuddled as she used the remote to switch the channel to Jerry Springer.

IT WAS an exclusive interview with Jasmin St. Clair, a porn queen who had had over three hundred men in ten hours. A "new world record," Jerry announced, although he wondered what kind of person would keep track of that sort of thing.

"What kind of person would participate in that?" Lynn asked from the couch.

"What kind of person would participate in that?" Jerry asked the audience from the studio somewhere.

"This definitely ain't real!" Carl said, interested. Sex interested him.

The girlfriend on the show was lambasting her boyfriend for taking part in that gang bang, while Jasmin sat around, self-satisfied, as Jerry couldn't keep his disgust under control.

She's a looker, he thought. Can't blame the guy.

"Would you do that, if you were there?" Lynn asked.

"Me? No," he said, shaking his head.

The announcement interrupted the show just as the producer of Jasmin's sex video had come onto stage. Carl's immediate thought when a man in a suit and tie, seated in a news booth with a grim look on his face, opened his mouth to say what he had to say, was that the producer bore an uncanny resemblance to Jerry Garcia of the Grateful Dead.

"LADIES AND gentlemen," the announcer said, with no identifying subtitles as to who he was. "This is not a test. This is real. The Chinese government has attacked us. Nuclear missiles are on their way here. This is not a test, I repeat, not a test. As I speak, right now, the first waves of megaton bombs and fusion bombs have hit Los Angeles and Seattle. I repeat, this is not a test. This is not a test. This is real. Please gather someplace safe. Please gather your loved ones and go someplace safe. Please gather your loved ones and go someplace safe."

THE TELEVISION showed static. Carl was sitting at the kitchen table, staring into space, thinking of nothing in particular. Lynn had gone next door to speak to her grandparents because the phone was out.

"There's only a cold 'whirr,'" she said, before she headed out next door to check. He wondered only how she knew it was cold.

"They're not there!" she said, frightened. "Davey isn't home either. The TV's on but nobody is home." She stood facing Carl as he slowly got up. She burst into tears, and he took her in his arms, wrapping them around her and holding her hard.

The rapture, he thought to himself, utterly sure, finally has come. Armageddon, Armageddon. The end is near. Hallelujah! Hallelujah!

He dismissed those thoughts right then and there for good.

"What are we gonna do? I'm so scared. What about mom and Stan?" she said, between sobs. He resolved to look fore more people in a while. He wanted to know if he was right. After getting all the provisions they'd need.

And what the hell was this? Why was Lynn here? If it were truly so, she should have been taken.

"Lynn," he said, holding her back a little. "Lynn, honey, I'm sure they'll be all right. Stan's a tough guy. He'll take care of her."

"You sure?" she said, between sniffles. "You sure of that?"

He wiped the tears streaming down her face with his hand, inwardly amazed at how warm they were. So different than snowflakes, he thought.

"Yes, I'm sure," he said, looking at her. "Trust me."

"Okay, but I'm really scared. Where's grandma and pawpaw?" she asked, shivering now, maybe going into shock. Cold doesn't do that to a person, he thought.

"Lynn, honey, let's go into the bedroom. Your mom's bedroom, okay?" he said, leading her.

"Why?"

He didn't answer, but once there, he started to throw things, dresses and boxes, out of the closet, which was pretty big, like a small bedroom. She caught on, and despite her fears and tears, she helped do what he ordered, emptying the closet, until it was completely empty.

"It's in the middle of the house, you know?" he said, as she listened, nodding. "We'll place the blankets and the heater in there, and I'm going to get a radio. You'll have to keep listening and checking the dial to get anything, whatever we can find, okay? I'm counting on you and your ears to do some magic, baby."

"Will this help? I mean, will all this help us?" she asked, waving her hands around the closet. "What about grandma and pawpaw?"

He grabbed the blankets off her mother's bed and placed them neatly onto the floor, spreading the corners. She stood by silently, watching him.

He knew she was watching but he finished what he was doing and then looked at her.

"Lynn, I'm going to go look for them, okay? Right after we do this. Okay, baby?"

"Okay, just be careful," she said.

"Okay. Let's get the rest of the blankets and the heater. Let's also hit the switchboard, and put all the electricity into one current heading into this room, okay? I want this place as dark as possible," he said.

"Why dark? Why not leave them on, so people can know we're here?"

Because this is when the loonies come out to play, he nearly shouted. "Because it's safer, baby. I want you warm and safe, okay? I'm gonna turn the heat up a bit, so you go grab whatever food you think we'll need for the time being, okay, baby?" he said, hugging her.

"Okay, take your jacket. I don't want you going out in that cold in that t-shirt, you hear?" she said authoritatively. He smiled. That's my girl, he thought.

THE HOUSES around his and Davey's were empty. There was a spilled glass of milk at Davey's, and he just knew. They were called home.

There was a shotgun under Davey's bed. Carl grabbed the gun and went next door to Jerry's. There he found the same thing. Empty. Like everyone was just in the next room, but empty. For good.

Jerry had a .32 revolver, and it was loaded. He had a box of cartridges nearby, so Carl stuffed those in his jacket pocket as well, and the .32 through his jeans' waistband.

He saw his image in the mirror. Jeans, work boots, open jacket, and hatless, showing his crew cut. You're in a world of shit, old boy. Time to go to work, he thought for no particular reason.

"Bang, bang," he said to his reflection, quietly.

HE TOOK a slow and careful walk around. It was very late, and he could feel vibrations on the ground. He saw bright yellow and red flashes to the south, where Charlotte lay. A tremor knocked him off his feet twice and he walked carefully after that, making sure his legs were loose and firm on the ground. He met nobody, heard nothing, except a consistent booming. A booming sound, much like a steady drumbeat. He had played football, and the team, being entirely deaf, used a drumbeat so they could know which beat to hike the ball to. He had never liked it himself, the drumbeats.

Lynn, he thought suddenly. And he ran home, frightened.

SHE WAS huddled under the blankets, listening to the radio in the middle of the room. They were wrapped around her, and she was still crying softly, less than she had been an hour, or was it hours, ago. He gave a sigh of relief, and after placing the revolver and shotgun nearby, her eyes widening at that, he went to his knees and hugged her hard.

"I love you, baby. You okay?" he asked.

"I'm okay. I love you. Are you okay?" she said.

"I'm okay, baby. I just want you safe."

"I'm okay, baby. I'm okay," she answered. "Did you feel those tremors, and can you hear those booms?" she asked, a small smile on her face. So sweet.

"Yeah, funny, huh?" he said, amazed at her resilience. She was handling it better than he thought she would.

"In a way, yeah. It sure is. I just hope we win," she said. "If it's really a war, I hope we, our side, get it over with."

"We will, you know. We're too big, too strong. I guess," he said.

"You find grandma and pawpaw?" she asked. He had no answer.

"It's okay," she said. "They're probably all visiting Hump or somebody." Hump was her great-grandfather. He lived on the other side of Lenoir.

"Probably, yeah," he said. She nodded and placed her head on his chest.

LATER, AFTER THE tremors subsided a little and the booming intensified, she asked about his parents. The question came unexpected. He hadn't thought about them at all.

"I'm sure Jason and Dad got everybody into the mountains. There's that little cabin Jason built. I'm sure they're right there at this moment," he said.

"I hope so," she said, after a moment. She looked very tired and worn.

"It's not like little green Chinamen are dropping out of the sky and going around attacking people," he said, after a moment of thought.

"Green?"

He chuckled. "So I got them mixed up with Martians. Little green men from Mars. 'Take me to your leader, huh'?"

She laughed.

"Chop Suey! We take back Bruce Lee, fish sticks, and Hideki Nomo!" He imitated a Chinaman saying, "Fu Manchu! No more wok soup for you, dirty American pig!"

"Stop that," she laughed. "You're so terrible, it's actually funny."

He smiled, holding her. The booming stopped, suddenly.

"Now it's quiet," he said. A boom came and then two more after that.

"Now it's not," he added as an afterthought, grinning.

Then the booming stopped, completely and suddenly, mid-crescendo.

"No more of that," he said matter-of-factly. He just knew. He didn't know how but he just knew.

Ten minutes had gone by, he noticed, looking at his watch. His still worked. Lynn's didn't. It had stopped the moment the announcements came. He found that strange, but hadn't found the need to bring it up.

Borrowed time, he thought. We're all on borrowed time.

"I love you, Carl Vandenberg. I love you with all my heart," she was saying quietly, holding him tight. She was crying a little. Tears were streaming gently down her face. He wiped them away. Row, row, row your boat, he thought, gently down the stream.

"Shhh, go to sleep," he said. They were face to face, and under the covers. With his free arm, he pulled the covers tight, up to their necks. Her breath was warm, and he held her tighter with the other arm. Hers were wrapped around him.

"Hold my hand," she said, and he complied.

"I love you, too, baby," he said in a while. Her eyes were closed.

"I love you," he repeated. She smiled and kissed him on the lips.

"I love you," she said.

"I love you," he said. "I love you, I love you, I love you. I love you. . ." he repeated, until he fell asleep, lost in the darkness and the warmth.

WHEN HE awoke, it was quiet and he could see a purple haze outside the window beyond the open doorway of the closet. There weren't any boomings or tremors, and he was alone. Lynn's clothes were there, as was her watch, lying where she had lain, next to him. She simply was gone and he knew, more strongly than ever, that she was now somewhere far more beautiful and safe.

Borrowed time, he thought.

LATER, AFTER HE ate a small bowl of Mueslix, he saw the electricity go out. It simply stopped, and a heavy fog rolled in. The snow was now purple, and he thought of Blowing Rock. So far away, and only yesterday.

He dressed warmly, put his sweatshirt hood up, and went out. The purple snow was just like the white snow, he thought. Only purple.

Probably radioactive, he told himself, grinning. He didn't go but a few feet away before he realized that he couldn't see the house. He quickly walked back, and it came into view.

He went back to the closet.

He placed the shotgun barrel into his mouth, and wondered if he should. He was terribly lonely and very afraid, on the verge of paralysis. Then he threw it away and started to cry. He missed Lynn.

HE ASSUMED it was night because he was so tired. His watch had stopped working a while ago. It read 7:35 and nothing more.

He slept, huddled under the blankets, frightened, walking in starts and jolts. He thought he saw his Uncle Barry rocking in his chair on the porch of the family farm. He thought he saw his mother and father, smoking cigarettes, huddled around the small table at the cabin Jason had built with his bare hands into Poplar Mountain, back in Kentucky. He dreamed he was playing a basketball game. The basketball game was unusual because he was thirteen years old, and everyone else was much older, and it was gently snowing goldfish. He could see them falling, oh so slowly, before disintegrating into nothingness. He saw Coach Crowe telling him to stop being a pussy and go out there and tackle that motherfucking South Carolinian player. He was dressed in a suit of armor, and Coach Crowe was wearing an astronaut's spacesuit. Yet all throughout he kept waking—waking and waking, only to have images flash into his mind. Then before he knew it, he was awake and looking out the window, watching the sky burst into terrible flashes of lightning and watching the purple snow fall and pile up a few feet beyond his line of vision. The fog was denser now, and he was very much alone.

He tried to read the Bible, but gave up after several attempts.

HE WAS rocking back and forth, thinking of nothing, on a kitchen chair, when he heard, or rather felt, a loud pop. Then he felt himself shiver. He forced himself to walk out onto the deck, dragging his feet through the pile of purple snow that had accumulated on the deck. He could see nothing but he knew, as the purple sky lightened up, that his time had come. The yellow glowing sun he could see now was coming, and he knew it was coming for him, and he could feel the snow melting and the hotness singeing his face. He felt the tears fall, and he saw them land on luxurious grass, in a far away place, splashing gently, and Lynn holding his face up, with a small welcoming smile, dressed in white and utterly beautiful. All was peace and love and grace, full of sunshine with baseballs hit into the sky, yellow kites in the air, competing against the wind along with a rainbow of colors over a green valley.

"Hail Mary! Hail Mary! Full . . ."

And he stood, fists raised, face upturned, feet firmly on the ground/deck/earth, standing his ground, making his stand, holding his ground and . . .

"of grace are thee . . ."

He felt his jacket melt away, white cotton laying gently across his body, his jeans catching fire, and Lynn kissing him on the cheek.

"One nation, under God . . ."

And he on her lips, raising his fists against a dying sun . . .

Hearing birds sing . . .

"Indivisible . . ."

Sibylle Gurtner May

SIBYLLE GURTNER MAY, who is hard of hearing, is the daughter of deaf parents. As a child, her mother told her to "look but never listen!" She took this advice to heart, and though she has learned to trust her hearing, she still prefers visual communication. May studied special education in college and now works with deaf and hard of hearing children. She has been writing poetry since she was twelve. In 1997, she co-edited, *Zwischentöne*, a collection of hard of hearing and hearing writers, writing on the theme of hearing—not hearing: where do I belong? This collection contains some of her poetry and short stories. May and her husband live in a village near Berne, Switzerland.

"if I could wish to hear well"

if I could
wish
to hear well

would it be
a gift?

      I would
      ride trains all day
      listen in on
      conversations beside me
      that I
      never understand

      I would
      learn to sing
      perhaps
      play the violin
      go to
      classical concerts

      I would
      learn languages
      passionately
      and rapidly
      German* above all   (*Englisch nicht moglich hier.)
      and Italian

would it be
a burden?

I would flee
because of the
noise everywhere

would be sleepless
because of constant sounds

would have
to learn
to hear anew

and:
where would I
belong?
a search
for
a new homeland

   look!

yes
listen!
no never
what for?
hearing always means
being able to
misunderstand too

seeing
sympathizing
is more precise
allows finer nuances
bears
inner knowing

Sotonwa Opeoluwa

Sᴏᴛᴏɴᴡᴀ Oᴘᴇᴏʟᴜᴡᴀ is a deaf poet, journalist, and playwright. He was born in Ijebu-Ode, Ogun State, Nigeria. He attended public primary and secondary local schools. After he became deaf at the age of sixteen, he had to abandon his schooling. Several years later, he learned of the Federal College of Special Education in Oyo, where he studied English and Education of the Hearing-Impaired. At the college, he was president of the Hearing-Impaired Student's Association, president of the Interpreter Club, editor-in-chief of *Audiowatch Magazine*, and editor-in-chief of the Campus Press Club. Opeoluwa is a strong advocate for deaf people's rights in Nigeria, and his writing reflects his concerns. He is currently attending law school at the University of Ilorin and is writing his autobiography.

The Victim of the Silent Void

Cast of Characters

OLD MAN	*Etiloba's father*
MAMA ETILOBA	*Etiloba's mother*
ETILOBA	*Deaf millionaire*
LARA	*Etiloba's first lover*
OWOLAFE	*Etiloba's wife*
BOWODE	*Etiloba and Owolafe's daughter*
TOSIN	*Etiloba and Owolafe's son*
GEORGE	*Owolafe's former classmate and lover*
MORIGBO	*Owolafe's friend*
FAGBAMILA	*Herbalist*
KEKE	*Physically handicapped interpreter*
OGURODIRAN	*Deaf drunkard*
ODIDIRE	*Deaf drunkard*
MAMA ELEMU	*Wine seller*
MAMA MALOMO	*Abiku's mother*
MALOMO	*Baby Abiku*
INTERPRETER	
ETILOBA'S UNCLE	
NEIGHBOR	

Prologue

If you can hear, then what?

If I cannot, then what?

Is it not the same God that made the cow with tail that also created the cow without tail?

If I am rich, then what?
If you are poor, then what?
Does it mean that fingers are equal?
If you are clever, then what?
If I am dull, then what?
Did the eternal painter ever paint our sense with equal color?
If you cheat me because I am deaf, you think nothing?
If you give me black for white because of my blindness, you think
    nothing?
If I help you and you pay me back with evil, you think nothing?
If you commend me in my presence and condemn me in my
    absence, you think nothing?
The unbiased and eternal Painter, perfect Creator, will surely see
    you and me through.
Anybody who, in this world, has half a loaf and a home in which
    to live,
Is no man's master and no man's slave.
Oh deafness, since the world's reality is illusion,
How long will you complain about this torment?
Resign your body to fate and put up with pain.
Because what the pen has written for you, it will not unwrite.
Oh you without knowledge, the corporeal shape is nothing.
And this dome of the nine charted spheres is nothing.
Take comfort, in the place of being and decay.
We are creatures of a single moment also nothing.
You have seen the world and all you saw was nothing.
And when you lurked at home, there was also nothing.
See what I've got from the world, nothing.
The fruit of my life's work? Nothing.
I am the light of the party, but when I sit down, I am nothing,
I am a wine-pot, but when I am broken, nothing.

ACT 1 SCENE 1

There are two chairs and a table on the stage. An old man walks in with a walking stick in his hand. He sits on one of the chairs.

OLD MAN: (*Coughs out loud.*) I know that my days are numbered by the Lord of heaven. (*Leans on the chair as if he wants to stand up, but suddenly puts away his walking stick.*) O Lord, dear God why, why did you do this? Why? You gave me wealth, houses. I have them in plenty. Cars? Different kinds in my garage (*suddenly stands up*). Hmm, what if I die? Who will manage all this fortune? You gave me only one son, but, to compound it all, the boy cannot hear, he is deaf. (*He sits down again, thinking; Mama Etiloba emerges from the back of the stage. She walks gently until she reaches her husband, who is lost in his thoughts. She touches him. He is startled, as if he has been sleeping.*)

MAMA ETILOBA: (*Exaggeratingly*) C-h-i-e-e-f-u-u. I cannot understand you nowadays. When things have become better, you refuse to eat well. You are always in a passive mood. Why, and what is really wrong?

OLD MAN: What is not wrong? Don't you know that we are the laughingstock of the whole community? A rich man indeed, with a useless child. Whenever I drive past, they point at me with pity and scorn me. They call me "Baba Aditi." Is that not worth worrying about? You see, it is better not to have a child at all than to have an incomplete, incoherent, completely useless, and handicapped child.

MAMA ETILOBA: (*Sympathetically.*) We cannot blame God; we just have to accept our fate. But Chief! If you will listen to me, you will not worry yourself any more.

Note. Dialogue in sign language between deaf characters appears in small capital letters. Words in the Yoruban language appear in italics. A glossary of Yoruban words appears on pp. 123–124.

OLD MAN: There she goes again. I am not abusing God, I am merely stating the obvious facts.

MAMA ETILOBA: B-a-b-a E-e-t-i-l-o-o-b-a-a. You will only kill yourself with hypertension. I have told you that we should marry him to a hearing girl. I think I have also discussed with you my plan to send Owolafe, the daughter of my gold-smith, to the Federal College of Special Education in Oyo, where she can learn how to communicate with 'Loba. The girl will surely make a good wife. She will also be able to help him run the family business when we are no more.

OLD MAN: I always say that to get a woman is not the problem for *pagoto*, but the problem lies in how to influence *pagoto*, the real swine in front of a pearl. You even made me remember what Mary Shelley wrote in her diary, "Teach him to think for himself." She said, "Oh, my God, teach him rather to think like other people." Deaf people are known to have their own ideology. They believe strongly in marrying one another, and to my understanding 'Loba is now dating a deaf lady. Do you now see the futility of your plan?

MAMA ETILOBA: (*Cuts in with a wave of her hand.*) Don't tell me that I don't know how I am going to control my son. My own son must not marry a deaf person. Never! Never! Never! In my life, eh, that is an impossibility.

OLD MAN: Hmm, the trouble with the world is that the stupid are cock-sure and the intelligent are taking the dose of life with a pinch of salt.

MAMA ETILOBA: Are you saying that I am too ambitious? If marriage can be arranged for two hearing people, why can't we arrange one between one deaf and one hearing person?

OLD MAN: Exactly! That is where my point lies. However, since you are sure of yourself, let me see how your plan and strategy will work.

MAMA ETILOBA: Hum, hum! The prick is boasting, the cunt is full of pride, then the battlefield is on the bed. (*She touches her breast.*) Unless Etiloba did not suck these breasts and I did not carry him for a full nine months in my womb, will he insist on what is contrary to my will? (*She exits.*)

Old man: There she goes again; who does not know that the cockroach will never be innocent at the assembly of fowls? (*He picks up his stick and walks away.*)

ACT 1 SCENE 2

Etiloba and Lara are sitting together. Both are deaf. Etiloba holds Lara's hand while Lara holds Etiloba's cheek. They are both lost in the love world. Suddenly, Etiloba changes his posture, as if he intends to do something. They communicate with each other in sign language while two voices interpret for them from the back of the stage.

LARA: CONFUSE. CONFUSE WHAT! WHAT!

ETILOBA: ME FACE PROBLEM, PROBLEM, BIG, BIG PROBLEM.

LARA: PROBLEM WHAT, PROBLEM WHERE, PROBLEM HOW?

ETILOBA: HOME, HOME PROBLEM BIG, FATHER; MOTHER GIVE PROBLEM, SERIOUS.

LARA: WHY? WHAT HAPPEN?

ETILOBA: BECAUSE YOU; FATHER, MOTHER, SAY NO, ME NOT MARRY DEAF.

LARA: YOU WANT MARRY HEAR? TERRIBLE! HEAR CHEAT, CHEAT, CHEAT YOU. TRULY, TO GOD, HEAR BAD, HEAR WICKED, HEAR NOT GOOD AT ALL; ME, NEVER, NEVER HEAR.

ETILOBA: ME SAME.

LARA: YOU SAME? LIE. BETTER TELL CLEAN, YOU WANT LEAVE ME, THAT IS WHY YOU NOT HAPPY. ME IDEA?

ETILOBA: PLEASE; MISUNDERSTAND NO, MISUNDERSTAND NO, TRUE TO GOD, ME LOVE YOU SERIOUS, YOU YOURSELF KNOW SERIOUS.

LARA: TALK! TALK! TALK! THINK ME FOOLISH? PLEASE LEAVE.

ETILOBA: LARA, NO-NO-NO, ME LOVE YOU VERY MUCH, TRUE TO GOD.

LARA: ME DON'T WANT YOUR MOTHER, FATHER KILL ME; BETTER LISTEN THEM AND MARRY HEAR.

ETILOBA: Never, never, me never marry hear; cheat me, cheat me. Not me.

LARA: You want your mother think me involved in your family problem? Not me, God will give me my deaf husband.

ETILOBA: God forbid! Me marry you. Finish.

LARA: No way! You marry hear. Finish.

ETILOBA: (*Becomes infuriated.*) Yourself not true love me. If mother talk say no and me say yes, you refuse say yes. If like misunderstand, your problem. (*Storms out in anger.*)

LARA: (*Downcast.*) Problem then understand. (*She sobs her heart out after Etiloba leaves and slowly walks away.*)

ACT 1 SCENE 3

Mama Etiloba is talking with Etiloba. The medium of expression is total communication. Mama Etiloba uses audible speech while a voice from backstage voices what Etiloba says to his mother.

MAMA ETILOBA: I am telling you that a hearing wife will do you good.

ETILOBA: Mama, leave me alone; I can never marry a hearing lady. Hearing people are robbers, cheaters, and deceivers, wicked and devilish fellows.

MAMA ETILOBA: You mean, I your mother am a deceiver? Have I ever deceived you before? Why should I then be deceiving my only son now? True, a hearing girl can interpret for you and for your visitor.

ETILOBA: (*Adamant.*) Mama, what you said is good, but she will dominate me and she will want to control my life. I don't want to marry a hearing lady. All I want is a deaf lady, like me, who can understand me better.

MAMA ETILOBA: (*Draws closer to him.*) You don't need to worry, I have found a good and humble lady for you.

ETILOBA: (*Aghast.*) For who?

MAMA ETILOBA: You think your mother is foolish? I am a good mother. (*She faces the audience and turns back to face Etiloba.*) For your information, I have paid the pride price on the lady.

ETILOBA: (*Becomes more infuriated.*) Without my consent?

MAMA ETILOBA: What do you mean? Let me tell you the facts: I have sent her to the Federal College of Special Education in Oyo, the only institution that has a special training program for teachers of the deaf, to learn your language.

ETILOBA: I don't believe you.

MAMA ETILOBA: Apart from this, I also am sending her to the state university, where she studies business administration so as to be useful for our business when your father is no more. So, you will be a blockhead not to marry such a person.

ETILOBA: So you have been doing this without my knowledge.

MAMA ETILOBA: Look here! Your father is ill and at the point of death. (*She exits.*)

ETILOBA: (*He starts to weep; he continues to sign while the interpreter voices for him.*) Why my Lord? Why should I fall a victim of the silent void? Where is the weft of my life's warp? In the circle of the Spheres, shadowed by deafness. Burnt and become dust, but where is the smoke? (*The lights fade.*)

ACT 1 SCENE 4

Etiloba sits alone thinking. Mama Etiloba emerges with Owolafe from the middle of the theater.

MAMA ETILOBA: Today, you will know your husband. He is a "been-to." You will know why I have been spending a lot of money on you.

OWOLAFE: I just don't know how I can thank you for all you have been doing for me. I have thought it best to marry him without any conditions.

MAMA ETILOBA: When you get to him, you must sign to gain his confidence. The more he understands you, the more he will be interested in you.

OWOLAFE: No problem, Mummy; I am an expert in sign language and I credit it to you for sending me to the Federal College of Special Education. There I learned that deaf people are not useless. There are even deaf lecturers who are better than their hearing counterparts. I still remember one deaf boy who graduated with us as the best overall student. In that school, there are also some blind lecturers. I even know one who was the dean of a whole school.

MAMA ETILOBA: *Akika!*

OWOLAFE: Even *aro* is the head of computer programming in the whole college.

MAMA ETILOBA: (*Surprised.*) It means nobody is useless.

They reach Etiloba on the stage. Owolafe makes a formal introduction to Etiloba in sign language and then interprets what Mama Etiloba says.

OWOLAFE: Good afternoon, sir.

ETILOBA: (*Startled.*) Good afternoon.

OWOLAFE: My name is Owolafe.

ETILOBA: You are welcome.

OWOLAFE: How is Gallaudet in America?

ETILOBA: (*Becomes suspicious.*) Fine.

MAMA ETILOBA: (*Faces the audience.*) This is what I want—somebody who can communicate with my son and be an intermediary between me and him. Am I not a good mother!

ETILOBA: (*Looks Owolafe in the face and is attracted to her beauty.*) How did you learn sign language and who taught you how to sign?

OWOLAFE: I went to Federal College of Special Education, where I studied deaf education.

ETILOBA: Oh! I see. I studied computer science at Gallaudet University in America.

OWOLAFE: I also earned my first degree in business administration from the state university.

ETILOBA: It is nice to meet you, and I believe that God has a purpose to fulfill in our lives. Our meeting here may not be altogether accidental. My mother told me all about you, but I thought it was all a dream.

MAMA ETILOBA: (*Interrupts them.*) I have concluded the arrangements for your wedding, and everything has been fixed right! (*Curtain falls.*)

ACT 2 SCENE 1

A man walks to the stage with a large card in his hand. On it is written AFTER FIFTEEN YEARS OF MARRIAGE. He walks around the stage dramatically displaying the board, to the amusement of the audience. After five minutes, he leaves the stage and walks out through the audience.

OWOLAFE: I told the manager to come see you because he is complaining that the materials sent to his company are not the ones they had ordered. He says they have no choice but to return the goods. In fact, he was talking in such a cruel manner that I think we should break our contract with him.

ETILOBA: My dear, you should know that this company has been working with our firm for a long time. When my father was still the manager, he instructed me to keep his agreement with this company. Despite the fact that he is no longer alive, we should not behave like that; rather, we should find some other means that we can use to pacify them so that our relationship will grow stronger.

TOSIN: (*Signing slowly and fingerspelling.*) Daddy, our teacher told us that there will be a PTA meeting in two weeks in the school. I have been given a letter from our school management that says they have decided to make you the chairman of our parent teacher association. (*Hands the letter to his father, who takes it and throws it on the table without reading it.*)

OWOLAFE: Etiloba, these people are very wise. I know that it is because they see you with lots of money and that we have put the world under our feet, so they now choose you as their chairman.

ETILOBA: Owolafe, don't talk like that. You know very well that whatever we have belongs to mankind. Yesterday, this money was my father's, but today the money is mine, and surely by tomorrow it will belong to our children. Therefore, we should not be selfish. Let us accept their offer, but you will be the one to accept the offer and stand in my behalf. Our society is moving at such a quick pace and the culture is fast changing. Who could predict that a deaf person could be bestowed such an honor?

OWOLAFE: I, myself, now realize the fact that deafness is not an insurmountable barrier to greatness.

ETILOBA: (*Cuts in.*) Yes, my dear, today we have many deaf lawyers, doctors, and business tycoons such as me. This is the Lord's doing. It is marvelous in our own eyes.

Bowode runs onto the stage shouting.

BOWODE: Daddy, Mommy, I am dead, I am finished. A man hit me with a *koboko*, saying my father is deaf and has made his son deaf because his son is my boyfriend. He said that the curse on my father has now been transmitted into his family through me.

ETILOBA: (*Worried.*) Oh my God, you are the maker of the hearing and the deaf people, Why is it that the humiliation is so great? If my wife goes to market, they rain abuses on her that she married a deaf man. If my children walk in the street, they are the laughingstock of the society. Why, my God?

OWOLAFE: Who is this man that is abusing my daughter? Bowode, let us go and meet the man. (*She places her arm across her daughter's shoulder and they walk off the stage, through the audience. The lights fade.*)

ACT 2 SCENE 3

Owolafe is walking on the stage. She is well dressed in traditional attire and wears a necklace that suits her outfit. She carries a bag that matches her head scarf.

OWOLAFE: He who says my husband is deaf, let him go to *Majidun* and die. I am proud to be the wife of a deaf person in this society.

George emerges from the opposite side of the stage. He wears a simple, secondhand shirt with rough trousers and bathroom slippers. He walks across the stage and nearly passes Owolafe.

GEORGE: Hey, excuse me madam; I do not mean to offend you, but if my question seems offensive, kindly forgive me.

OWOLAFE: What is this all about?

GEORGE: Nothing, but it seems I know you from somewhere. I just can't remember from where. (*He knocks his head to try to remember.*) Oh yes, did you go to the state university at all?

OWOLAFE: Of course. Yes, I am an alumna of the great state university.

GEORGE: Exactly then! You must be Owolafe, who I knew in the Department of Business Administration.

OWOLAFE: Yes, that is my department.

GEORGE: Don't you recognize me? I am your old friend George from school.

OWOLAFE: (*Examining the man, she suddenly recognizes him.*) George, is that you?

GEORGE: Yes, dear, I am your George.

OWOLAFE: I never expected to meet you in this way at all. You, a graduate of a university, wearing second-class clothes and bathroom slippers. Why?

GEORGE: It is not my own fault. I have been moving from one place to another in search of work. Despite the fact that I have my degree, I have remained without a job. Even day-to-day living has become very hard for me. The worst is that my father has sent me out of the house, insisting that I must find a job because he cannot continue to support me.

OWOLAFE: (*Deeply moved.*) I did not know that you had been passing through all this agony, but you need not worry anymore. Now that I have met you, I will try my best for you. But mind you, our love of old is now dead. I am now married to a business tycoon, and we have two children. But because of the love I still have for you, I will talk to my husband to help you with some money so that you can embark on a business that will fetch you a good profit.

GEORGE: (*Downcast.*) You mean you are married? Do you know that since we left school I have never had any wife because I was hoping to see you one day? But since the situation is like this, there will be no problem. But please, please, let me meet your husband so that I can thank him if truly he will help me.

OWOLAFE: You need not see him because he is deaf, and I am the only person that understands his language. But try and meet me on Friday, next week, at this very place.

GEORGE: Okay. Thank you very much. But please, don't disappoint me. Please let me see you.

OWOLAFE: No problem. I will see you then. (*She exits.*)

GEORGE: Oh what is all this? The woman whom I have nursed the hope of marrying is now married to a deaf man! A deaf man! Is this a joke? I must see to it that she comes back to me. I cannot afford to lose my girlfriend to a mere deaf man. What can I do? Hmm. Yes, I know what I am going to do. I must go to meet Baba Fagbamila for advice and Juju. I know that the man will help me out of my dilemma. (*The lights fade.*)

ACT 3 SCENE 1

On old man with grey hair sits on the stage. He is an herbalist. He is chanting in the Yoruba language in a loud, coarse voice. He is surrounded by different kinds of paraphernalia. A woman runs on to the stage with a baby.

MAMA MALOMO: (Crying.) *Baba o, E gba mi o.*

FAGBAMILA: (*Snatches the baby from the woman.*) What is it? So, this baby refuses to stop all these convulsions. You don't know anything. *Abiku*, you are playing with fire.

MAMA MAMOLO: Please *baba*, don't allow him to die this time around. This is the fifth time I have brought him to you.

FAGBAMILA: Did you ever mutilate his body when he was in a coma?

MAMA MALOMA: Yes. Baba Fatoki of Oke Ona did it for him when he died last time.

FAGBAMILA: When he was born, did you see any marks on his body?

MAMA MALOMO: Baba, look at the rib and the ankle (*shows Fagbamila some marks on the baby's body*). It is all that the man did when he died last time, and when I gave birth to him again, all the marks were there on his body.

FAGBAMILA: I can now see clearly. Look here (*holds the baby and talks directly to him*), you have to stay this time. (*Malomo cries.*)

FAGBAMILA: *Omode ko'mo Ogun, On'pe l'efo. Mo ni eyi t'aba wi fun ogbo l'ogbo ngbo. Eyi t'aba wi fun Ogba l'ogba n'gba. Ma yii pada l'oni ko maa lee yii ohun emi Fagbamila pada.* Will you stay? (*Malomo cries out even more.*) You, this riddle of the palm. The digger of misfortune. The woes for the mother. You are a thief and I have caught you red-handed today. You can't escape from my hand. Fire that smites the forest when it is wet is in my amulet. Woman, do not panic. Since the child is in my hand, there is no cause for alarm.

MAMA MALOMO: (*Sobs.*) Please, help me to beg him to stay. The milk in my breast has gone sour. Please Baba, help me to convince him that his father and mother love him and we shall do everything to make his life comfortable.

FAGBAMILA: Don't worry. I know what to do. Hmm. *Agbekude* is the answer to his problem. You will have to buy some materials for the ritual, which I must perform at midnight when the congregation of *Abiku* is on the round table. It is only in that meeting that I shall force him to renounce his membership. Because if he does not renounce his membership, all efforts will always prove futile.

MAMA MALOMO: What are the things I am going to buy?

FAGBAMILA: One white ram without blemish. We shall use it to appease the congregation of *Abiku* so that they will not trouble him after he has renounced his membership. And seven hundred naira for the sacrifice to the queen of the coast, who is the maker and the giver of *Abiku* children.

MAMA MALOMO: I shall bring everything as soon as possible, but what will you do for him so that he will not go before the materials are ready?

FAGBAMILA: (*He chants some silent incantations and gives the baby back to his mother.*) He will never go with the word of my mouth. But be cautious. He heard what I told him, and he promised to stay for another twenty-one days. Should you fail to bring the items before twenty-one days lapse, he will die.

MAMA MALOMO: Thank you, Baba. I will do as you have said (*exits with the baby*).

FAGBAMILA: *Ifa jinginrindin, Ifa mo gbo oro kan, Ifa jinginrindin o, Ifa mo gbo oro kan* . . . . (*A voice is heard from the back of the stage.*)

GEORGE: (*Off stage.*) *A ago onile o, Baba o, the arole* of Orunmila. The great hunter in the wilderness of wizards. The mastermind of peace where it seems there will be no peace. The great sailor who is sailing in the ocean called life. You have dined with Olugbon, you have dined with Aresa, and at the end you were made the king of all wizards. *Baba o*, any witch who refuses to succumb to the power of Fagbamila becomes a thing of history. Any wizard who grows horns overnight finds himself ensnared in the trap of Fagbamila. (*George walks onto the stage.*)

FAGBAMILA: *Orunmila a gbe o.* Orunmila will help you. All the sixteen demons that are governing this territory will help you. It is now a long time since we have seen each other. I think your work has now become a thing of possibility. I can see it myself. Orunmila is telling me. But *Aki saju eleede pe ede*, whatever might be your problem, tell Ifa and Orunmila shall interpret it for you. (*He offers George some palm kernels for divination. George, in turn, talks silently to the kernels and then puts them down along with $5). Ifa Olokun, asoro dayo, Iwo lawo o emi lo gberi, Ma fibi pe ire o, ma si fi Ire pe Ibi. Bo ba seri gan ni ko wi o.* (*Fagbamila picks up the kernels and throws them down.*) Oh! Oh! I can see the very man who is troubling you. You have a great task to accomplish, but this is a cursed man whose horns resemble the tusks of an elephant, whose eyes shine like the face of a lion. To kill him will amount to your death. I saw him; a man from the silent world whose ears have been sacrificed to the queen of the cape coast, who in turn has made him rich, a great man in the business world.

GEORGE: Baba, you have seen everything. Ifa sees it, Orunmila knows it. This is the dilemma I am facing. My fiancée is married to another man and the worst is that the man is deaf. I cannot imagine losing a woman whom I love to a mere deaf man. I want that woman to come back to me because she is the only person in my life. Let the man die, let him die like a common fowl. After all, what is he? Just a deaf and dumb man. I want to kill this man.

FAGBAMILA: My son, what I have seen in front of Orunmila shows that it is impossible. This man is indeed a warrior. If you attempt to get rid of him, it will only amount to your downfall.

GEORGE: Hey! Baba, please just help me out. I need this woman back in my life.

FAGBAMILA: Ifa warns you; desist, desist and beware, lest the man favors you and turns a big calamity upon you. I can see that the man is going to help you. Therefore, do not harm him.

GEORGE: Baba, please, whatever it will cost me, I will give you.

FAGBAMILA: *Ifa ni ma see l'ogun matee.* I will never use my hand to shed the blood of an innocent man.

GEORGE: Since you cannot do it, Baba, I am off. (*He exits.*)

ACT 3 SCENE 2

Etiloba's house. Etiloba and Owolafe are chatting in sign language.

OWOLAFE: We need to help that boy. Please. He was my class-mate in the university. I was moved when I saw him because he was always helping me when we were in school. Please help him with some money to establish a business.

ETILOBA: There is no problem. When we use our money to help the helpless and give to the needy, we are doing what the Lord in heaven wants us to be doing. I will not only help him, but I will also make sure he manages the business judi-ciously. By the way, how much do you think we should give the man?

OWOLAFE: I think three million will be enough for his busi-ness.

ETILOBA: (*Takes out his checkbook and writes a check for three million naira.*) Here it is; tell him to go to the bank and start his business with it immediately. (*Hands the check to Owolafe, who immediately takes it.*)

OWOLAFE: Thank you. (*The lights fade.*)

ACT 4 SCENE 1

George is standing at the edge of the stage, talking to himself.

GEORGE: I have been waiting since morning without seeing Owolafe.

OWOLAFE: (*Enters.*) George, I am very sorry for keeping you waiting. It is because I was talking about your need, as I promised.

GEORGE: I am not angry.

OWOLAFE: (*Hands the money to George.*) This is my promise. It is a check for three million naira. Do not bother to thank me. I am going. (*She turns to go, but George calls her back.*)

GEORGE: You can't leave like that. I will ever be grateful for what you have done for me, but . . . (*pausing a little before continuing*) I would love it if you would listen to a story I heard. It is the mystery behind the success of a deaf millionaire.

OWOLAFE: What would that be? Is it because of the money I gave to you that you thought of such a thing?

GEORGE: No, but from my understanding, your husband entered into a treaty with the demon of deafness. As soon as you have five children for him, you will all become deaf.

OWOLAFE: (*Opens her mouth in amazement.*) You mean . . . who told you that? I never heard such a legend, but today I am sure you are up to something. You must be nursing a hidden agenda.

George: I don't think so. I had to tell you because I love you, so that you can escape for your dear life. If I didn't love you, I would have allowed it to happen. For your own safety, it is better you escape, escape for your life.

OWOLAFE: (*Downcast and confused.*) Then how do you think I can do that since you know that I love my husband.

GEORGE: Sit down here. If his family will not leave you alone, kill one of your children and lie to his family that he beats all of you. Say that in the process of beating, the child died because he could not hear her cries. Nobody will believe him when he denies this since you are the only person who understands his language. That will work.

OWOLAFE: I don't know how I can handle this, but I will give it some thought, and I will let you know my final decision. I will give you my address so that you can check on me at home. George, do you believe that our old love is not yet dead, despite the fact that I am married? The way you are speaking makes me remember your tender touch and caress, especially when we made love.

George: Yes, the love is still burning in me, but let us get rid of this man and we shall see what we can do. (*The lights fade.*)

ACT 4 SCENE 2

The curtain opens on an old-fashioned Elemu Shop. Empty kegs of wine and empty bottles are scattered on the floor. Two men are on stage. They communicate with each other in sign language while two interpreters voice for them at the front of the stage. Mama Elemu is washing the empty kegs and calabashes.

ODIDIRE: THIS WINE SWEET, SWEET, STRONG, SHARP. TRUE ME LOVE THIS.

OGURODIRAN: BETTER TELL MAMA BRING GOOD WINE TOMORROW, TOMORROW, SAME YESTERDAY, NOT SWEET. (*He waves his hand to get Mama Elemu's attention and explains in local sign language what they are talking about.*)

MAMA ELEMU: (*Raises her hands up, signs and speaks.*) YOU MEAN THIS WINE BE STRONG? MAKE YOU NO WORRY. I GO KEEP FINE, FINE, WINE FOR YOU EVERYDAY.

OGURODIRAN: (*Points to Mama*). YOU GOOD, GOOD. (*Turns to talk to Odidire.*) ME PREPARE MARRY HEAR. TRUE ME THINK YOU WRONG. YOU MARRY DEAF AND ADVISE ME TO MARRY DEAF? NOT ME! ME SELF WIFE DEAF, HOW AND WHY?

ODIDIRE: FOOLISH YOU! ME EXPLAIN, EXPLAIN NOW. YOU NOT LISTEN, LATER YOU REGRET; YOU WILL SEE. HEAR BAD, BAD, TRUE, TRUE; HEAR CHEAT, CHEAT YOU AND ESCAPE. NOT SEE SAMSOM, FINISHED SCHOOL IN AMERICA COME BACK TO NIGERIA AND MARRY HEAR. WHAT HAPPEN? HEAR JUMP, JUMP. LIE! LIE! DECEIVE! DECEIVE! DECEIVE! CHEAT! CHEAT! TROUBLE! TROUBLE! PEACE NO.

OGURODIRAN: NOT ALL, DEAF SAME! SEE CHIEF ETILOBA. HE MARRY HEAR, ENJOY, ENJOY RICH MORE, MORE POPULAR BIG. YOU THINK IF HE MARRY DEAF HE CAN? FUNNY, HE CAN'T.

ODIDIRE: YOU NOT SEE "FATHER OF ALL DEAF IN NIGERIA." WIFE CAN'T COOK, CAN'T WASH. HE SELF POPULAR AND INTELLIGENT BUT HOME PEACE NO, YOU THINK? ETILOBA ENJOY? FUNNY YOU. HIS MONEY MAKE THAT HEAR STAY. TRUE, ME KNOW, JUST WAIT. ETILOBA WILL SUFFER TRUE, TRUE, ME PROPHESY.

OGURODIRAN: YOU WANT TELL ME THAT, THAT HEAR MARRY ETILOBA BECAUSE MONEY? ME NOT BELIEVE.

ODIDIRE: YOU THINK BECAUSE ETILOBA HAVE PEACE WITH HEAR, ALL SAME?

OGURODIRAN: ME TELL YOU EQUAL EQUAL.

ODIDIRE: (*Sips and puts the cup down.*) ONE THING YOU NOT KNOW IS THAT IF YOU HAVE FOOD, MONEY, PEOPLE HELP HELP UNTIL YOU FINISH. IF FINISHED, PEOPLE QUIT, QUIT, LEAVE YOU ALONE. YOU SUFFER, SUFFER.

OGURODIRAN: ME KNOW YOU WELL. YOU ALWAYS TALK PROVERB PROVERB. GOOD KING SOLOMON.

ODIDIRE: ME SELF KNOW YOU CAN'T LISTEN; TRUTH BITTER BITTER. (*George walks into the shop.*) YOU JUST WAIT; MY PROPHESY HAPPEN. (*George looks at the two men angrily.*) YOU THINK? FOOLISH MAN.

GEORGE: (*Talks to Mama Elemu.*) Why do you allow these nugatory elements to come in here? Don't you know they embarrass your customers?

MAMA ELEMU: Sorry Oga, I don't know what I can do to scare

them away. All the best wine I have got has been finished by those good-for-nothings. (*Morigbo enters.*) Here comes the most glamorous woman of our century.

MORIGBO: How is your business? (*She sees the two deaf man and raises her eyebrows in disdain.*) So these useless fellows go spoil all your business. I tell you to say they're not fit to drink in this shop. Na, so you then allow them in.

MAMA ELEMU: Please, leave them alone. They are good and nice now. Why all these insults toward them? Don't you see Etiloba, who is chief and deaf? He is very kind and generous. (*George looks up on hearing Etiloba's name.*)

MORIGBO: You know that the man's wife, Owolafe, is my friend, and she is too much in love with her deaf and know-next-to-nothing husband.

GEORGE: You see Mama, they have spilt my wine. You must replace it or else I will not pay.

MAMA ELEMU: Sorry my husband. (*She brings George another full cup of wine.*)

GEORGE: (*Speaks to Morigbo.*) Madam, I wish to see you because I have an important message to give to your friend Owolafe.

MORIGBO: Is there a problem?

GEORGE: There is a big problem ahead of her.

MORIGBO: What is it all about?

GEORGE: I am the messenger of the truth from the abode of I AM THAT I AM.

MORIGBO: What is your message from the great God?

GEORGE: I AM sent me to tell you to advise Owolafe that if she has five children for that man called Etiloba, they will become deaf.

MORIGBO: Is that so?

GEORGE: Yes.

MORIGBO: That is good for her. I have been telling her, but she will never listen. Let it happen to her. She even understands sign language. Therefore, she doesn't have any problems.

GEORGE: I AM insists that she must go back to her former boy-friend so as to avert the wrath of Eledumare.

MORIGBO: I cannot tell her because it is not my business.

GEORGE: I AM told me to give you five thousand naira to do the work (*hands her some money*).

MORIGBO: Thank God. I have been languishing in poverty, and I AM has seen my plight. I shall try my best for I AM, the great and divine provider.

ACT 4 SCENE 3

Morigbo and Owolafe are on stage, playing a game of Ludo.

MORIGBO: I have told you that five-to-one I gave you yesterday must be doubled today, but you think I am joking.

OWOLAFE: Even if you beat me here, you cannot beat me in busi-ness. You may win at Ludo, but still I am your better in other things.

MORIGBO: You think because your husband is rich and mine is poor, you are better than me? Sit there with that cursed man. He offended the gods; that is why he cannot hear, and you will reap the consequences soon.

OWOLAFE: (*Shocked.*) Morigbo, how true is this fact? I learned that if I have five children for him, we will all become deaf.

MORIGBO: Exactly. I have been careful not to tell you so that you will not think I want to snatch your husband. I even dreamed God insisted you must go back to your former boyfriend to avert the wrath.

Owolafe looks downcast. The light fades.

ACT 4 SCENE 4

Etiloba's house. George and Owolafe are being playful, kissing each other.

OWOLAFE: George, you are still sweet like the olden days. I cannot forget all our love-making. You have proved you are still the same. The man I live with is deadwood that I must first put in the sun before he can give me fire.

GEORGE: (*Caressing her.*) Dear, don't talk like that. I told you, let us get rid of this man and believe we shall marry each other. (*They kiss again.*)

Keke, a physically disabled interpreter, enters.

KEKE: What are you doing and who is this man?

OWOLAFE: (*Shocked.*) He is my uncle from the village. We have not seen each other for a long time; that is why we are sharing our joy.

KEKE: Will you be kissing your uncle, in your husband's house?

OWOLAFE: Yes! That is how we behave in our community.

KEKE: Well, that is good, but please, where is Chief Etiloba?

OWOLAFE: He has gone on a business trip to Germany.

KEKE: When will he return?

OWOLAFE: I think in two weeks time.

KEKE: Okay, I will see him then; we have business to discuss.

OWOLAFE: Okay.

KEKE: Bye-bye.

GEORGE: Don't mind that silly useless, handicapped person. They are all in the same position.

George coaxes Owolafe down on the floor and they begin to make love. The lights fade.

ACT 5 SCENE 1

Keke is signing and talking with Etiloba. They look serious.

KEKE: I came to your house two weeks ago and I saw your wife with a man in your parlor. They were kissing and caressing each other. I asked Owolafe who the man was. She said that he was her uncle. How can your wife be kissing an uncle?

ETILOBA: I have often seen the man, but Owolafe tells me that they are relatives. Whenever I watch them closely, I always suspect that something is going on between them. But since I am deaf, nobody can help me at all.

KEKE: Don't let her know now, but we should plan how to catch her.

ETILOBA: What do you think I can do?

KEKE: I will give you a pocket cassette recorder. When you notice that they are coming, put the recorder under the table and pretend not to notice them. After that, I will tell you the next step.

ACT 5 SCENE 2

Etiloba is sitting in his house while George and Owolafe are talking in another room. Etiloba takes out a small tape recorder and, without being noticed, he puts a blank cassette in it and pretends he is searching for something.

GEORGE: I never knew that a deaf man could be so rich.

OWOLAFE: He is rich, but let us kill Bowode. I shall tell people that he beat the child until she died.

ETILOBA: (*Signing.*) Who is that man?

OWOLAFE: I have told you; he is my uncle. What else do you need now? (*Turns away from her husband.*)

GEORGE: You need to act quickly before people start to suspect us.

OWOLAFE: But let's go and spend tonight at the Sheraton Hotel so that we can enjoy each other.

GEORGE: What will you tell your husband?

OWOLAFE: I will him that my cousin is very sick in the village, and you came to tell me that my presence is urgently needed.

GEORGE: What if he tells you that he will go with you?

OWOLAFE: I know what I will say, I am not a kid. (*Turns to Etiloba and begins to sign and talk.*) Chief, I was told that my cousin is very sick in the village and that my presence is urgently needed. I would ask you to follow me, but it will be better if I go alone now and come back tomorrow morning.

ETILOBA: (*Draws out his wallet and offers her some money.*) Give this money to your family in the village and extend my greetings to everybody.

OWOLAFE: (*Stands up with George to go.*) Thank you, bye-bye. (*Owolafe and George exit.*)

Etiloba runs to where he put the tape recorder, removes the cassette, and puts it in his pocket. Keke comes in.

KEKE: Where is your wife, Chief? I overheard the whole conversation from my hiding place, but I want to play the tape recording so I can interpret it to you.

Etiloba takes out the recorder and puts the cassette in it. As the tape plays, Keke interprets.

TAPE RECORDER: I never knew that a deaf man could be so rich. He is rich, but let us kill Bowode. I shall tell people that he beat the child until she died. (*Pause.*) I have told you; he is my uncle. What else do you need now? You need to act quickly before people start to suspect us. But let's go and spend tonight at the Sheraton Hotel so that we can enjoy each other. What will you tell your husband? I will tell him that my cousin is very sick in the village and you came to tell me that my presence is urgently needed. What if he tells you that he will go with you? I know what I will say, I am not a kid. Chief, I was told that my cousin is very sick in the village and that my presence is urgently needed. I would ask you to follow me, but it will be better if I go alone now and come back tomorrow morning.

ETILOBA: Are you interpreting the cassette or are you telling me something different?

KEKE: I am telling you what the cassette says.

ETILOBA: That is not the truth, but I will keep this cassette because what Owolafe told me is different. She told me that one of her cousins is sick and she has to go down to the village to see him.

KEKE: She lied.

ETILOBA: We have been married for fifteen years, and she has been a trustworthy wife all these days. Why would she change at the very moment we are enjoying our wealth? I doubt it.

KEKE: Chief, keep the cassette. If you don't believe me, time will tell.

ACT 5 SCENE 3

Owolafe walks on stage crying, carrying her dead daughter. Etiloba wonders what has happened.

OWOLAFE: Yee!!! My neighbor, come and see. Oh, my husband has killed my daughter. He beat the girl 'til she died.

NEIGHBOR: (*Consoling her.*) Don't worry. Stop crying.

Etiloba's uncle runs on to the stage.

ETILOBA'S UNCLE: (*Pointing an accusing finger at Etiloba.*) See, you have killed your child with your bare hands, and now you should go and cook her and eat her.

OWOLAFE: No, no; he cannot change. This is not the first time he has beaten us mercilessly. I cannot bear the pain again.

ETILOBA'S UNCLE: Please don't do that.

ETILOBA: (*Turns to the audience.*) So, what Keke told me is true. (*He breaks into tears, realizing that people have shown him respect to his face but actually have taken advantage of him. The lights fade.*)

ACT 6 SCENE 1

Two months have passed. Etiloba sits in the dining room, reading the newspaper. Owolafe comes in with a dish of food in her hand.

OWOLAFE: I have brought your food. It is better you take it now because it is still hot.

ETILOBA: What about you?

OWOLAFE: I have eaten mine and I am satisfied.

ETILOBA: If you love me, let us eat it together.

OWOLAFE: Do you mean to tell me that since we have married, it is at this time you no longer trust my love? If you can't eat it alone, leave it there. (*Etiloba picks up the dish and leaves the room. Owolafe turns to the side.*) What is wrong? Who has revealed my plan? Who might have revealed it to him?

Etiloba, Keke, the neighbor, and Etiloba's uncle enter with the food.

ETILOBA: Today we are going to learn who killed my daughter and who your uncle who comes from the village really is, along with what you have put in the food.

OWOLAFE: What do you mean by that? I cannot even tolerate all this. I shall pack my things and get out of your house; I'll leave you alone with your woe.

NEIGHBOR: Owolafe don't do that; let us settle the problem.

OWOLAFE: No, no. I cannot stay with all these insults from this deaf wizard. (*She exits; the curtain falls.*)

ACT 6 SCENE 2

George is sitting comfortably in his office, which consists of a table and two chairs. He is writing when Owolafe enters.

GEORGE: Ah! Owolafe, welcome. How are you today? I have not seen you for quite a long time. Why?

OWOLAFE: George, it is difficult, difficult, very difficult. It is not possible. Etiloba refused to eat that food. In fact, I have fought it to the end.

GEORGE: (*Interested.*) And what then is the man up to, and what is your next step?

OWOLAFE: What should I do? I have left his house, but since you have already built one, there is no cause for alarm. I shall move in with you.

GEORGE: (*Surprised.*) No, no, no; you still have to settle the matter. (*Pauses.*) Well you know, Owolafe, I've had something on my mind all these days, but now I must tell you because I cannot continue with two women. Do you know that my wife is pregnant? I cannot marry two women!

OWOLAFE: What! What! What do you mean, are you dreaming?

GEORGE: No, I am telling you the whole truth.

OWOLAFE: That cannot be.

GEORGE: You can believe it or not. The fact is that you must stop coming to my house from now on.

OWOLAFE: George, are you out of your senses?

GEORGE: I am not mad, only tired of your love.

OWOLAFE: But, but. You asked me to kill my daughter, and I did so. Then you told me to kill my husband, but it was impossible. Now you are saying that you cannot marry me?

GEORGE: That is the whole truth.

OWOLAFE: George, look at me from head to toe. I will show you. I will show you. I will let you know that I am really an Ijebu woman. If that woman is your new joy, when you get to hell you will know the difference, and you will account for your deeds.

GEORGE: You think you can kill me? (*Laughs.*) Let me tell you, I have bathed in the sea of *Orisa nla*. I have swum in the ocean of *Agbekude*. No one can kill me except the will of Olodumare. I have become a bone that my captor can neither swallow nor throw away. (*The lights fade.*)

ACT 6 SCENE 3

Etiloba signs while Keke interprets for him.

ETILOBA: Listen my people. Is it a curse that I am born to be deaf? The society rejects us. See, my wife became unfaithful. She brought a lover to my house, yet told a lie that the man was her uncle. See, she killed her daughter just to get rid of me. See, she puts poison in my food just to kill me and get away with my money. This is real agony. The bereavement in my soul, the anguish is ruining me within. Thanks to the Almighty God who saved me from this evil woman. My people, I cannot hear, but listen to this tape recording. I believe you will learn some lessons from it.

Owolafe enters. When she hears her voice on the recording and realizes her secret is out, she falls on the ground and starts weeping. Neighbors and family open their mouths in wonder.

OWOLAFE: Ha, had I known. Please, eh, eh (*gets on her knees*), forgive me. It is the work of the devil. George deceived me. He was the one who asked me to kill my daughter. Ha! (*Cries.*) I gave him three million naira for his own business—money that belonged to my husband. He ordered me to kill my husband so that I could marry him. But Etiloba refused to eat the food that I had poisoned. Yes, that food before you (*pointing to the food*), there is poison in it. And now the man cheated my husband and cheated me. He impregnated another woman and then told me that he was no more in need of me. Ha! I must die, but before I die, George must die.

ETILOBA: (*Faces the audience.*) My people, can you see for yourself the danger and the repercussions of marrying someone imposed by one's parents? You may think that deaf people who marry each other are insane, but I tell you, they have more peace than the so-called intermarriage couple. Nothing is gained until you become deaf to understand. Nothing is gained until you follow the path of one in utter darkness. Nothing is gained unless tears of blood wash your cheeks. Why the inflamed desire? Nothing is gained until you and I are left free to become whatever we choose to be. (*The curtain falls.*)

EPILOGUE

Those who dominate the Circle of learning and culture
Make themselves perfect and become a lamp among their peers.
By daylight they cannot escape from darkness,
So they tell a fable about my deafness and go to sleep.
"The evil that men do live after them," said Shakespeare.
He who destroys others so as to succeed
Must have destruction awaiting him
At the gate of his own success.
Leviticus, chapter nineteen verse fourteen says:
"You shall not curse the deaf,
Nor put a stumbling block before the blind."
Alas! Deaf people have become the object of ridicule,
Laughingstocks in the society.
Ha! This is man's inhumanity to man,
A total misconception of what deafness entails.
My creator! Why hast thou made me deaf?

Why hast thou put me in this shoe?
Why do you want me to sail through the ocean of the world
   soundlessly?
I know being and "non-being" outward form.
I know every exaltation and depression's inwardness,
With all this knowledge, may I be ashamed
To know my stage beyond deafness.
If my coming here were my will, I would not have come.
If my deafness were my will, I would have rejected it.
If my departure were my will, how should I go?
Nothing could be better on this ruined lodging
Than not to have come, not to be . . . . not to go.

GLOSSARY OF YORUBA PHRASES

Abiku: A baby who has convulsions

Agbekude: A juju chain that is prepared to ward off unwanted and untimely death in children who are having convulsions.

Akika: Wonderful

Aki saju eleede pe ede: "Don't be too forward."

Aresa: The son of Olugbon

Aro: Someone who is physically disabled

Baba o, E gba mi o: "Father, please save me!"

Eyi t'aba wi fun Ogba l'ogba n'gba: "It is what we give a collector that he will take."

Ifa jinginrindin: "Invincible Oracle."

Ifa mo gbo oro kan: "Oracle! I heard something."

Ifa ni ma see l'ogun matee: "Ifa says don't do it; it is the only antidote for not bringing shame."

Ijebu: A town in Ogun State in Nigeria

Koboko: A refashioned horse tail used by natives of Yoruba land to beat (whip) their children

Majidun: A river located in a suburb of Lagos

Ma yii pada l'oni ko maa lee yii ohun emi Fagbamila
    pada: "Irrevocability is the medicine that turned the word of me, Fagbamila, into irrevocable."

Olugbon: A legendary Yoruba king who was believed to be wiser than all the inhabitants of the world

Omode ko'mo Ogun, On'pe l'efo "It is ignorance that made a child mistake poison for food."

Orunmila: A god of the Ifa Oracle in Yoruba land

Orunmila a gbe o: "Orunmila will help you."

Pagoto: Someone who refuses to appreciate the honor and prestige bestowed on him. Instead, he pursues a cause that eventually leads to his downfall.

The arole of Orunmila: The intercessor for Orunmila

Douglas Bullard

Douglas Bullard is the author of the novel *Islay*, which is about a deaf state. He graduated from Gallaudet University in 1964 and worked in Alaska as a geologist for many years. He now lives in retirement in Florida.

Yet: Jack Can Hear!

How is a boy to learn who he really is
without discarding who he is not?

LAURENT CLERC

ON HIS RETURN to the school from yet another bout with surgery during the summer, Jack had to sleep flat on his back, just as at the hospital, and stare at car headlights swinging across the ceiling, just as at the hospital, too. He'd much rather sleep on his side, his feet tucked up closer to the warmth of his torso, his arms folded around the pillow, except that his new ears were uncomfortable when rested upon the pillow, and sometimes hurt the side of his head. And he was afraid they'd break or tear off and blood would spurt out.

His mother had told him to be very careful with his new ears because they were very expensive. Gripping him by the shoulders, she'd said they were his only hope of ever becoming a normal hearing boy that nobody would ever laugh at anymore. And she emphasized they were real ears, not cheap hearing aids. Then, she'd softly stroked his hair, his cheek, his eyebrows, and the back of his neck, careful not to touch the ears for they did feel funny to the touch, kind of repulsive to the finger, cold as the waxy skin of a cadaver, somewhat like the latex membrane of surgeon's gloves. She'd touched them once, just once, when he was wheeled out of surgery in a deep coma from the anesthesia. They felt so cold she nearly cried out that he was dead.

And the color wasn't quite right. It was all one shade of beige, almost like surgical tubing, unlike the subtle shadings from pink to tanned, pale to flush, of living ears. The beige had an unnatural light to it, as if the ears had been microwaved in a tanning salon.

Yet: Jack can hear! Jack can hear! He really could hear! The ears worked! The operation was completely successful! The patient did not die!

Dr. Bangs was immensely pleased. He'd finally achieved the stratosphere of a Jesus Christ. All the years of hard work and experimenting with cadavers and mice and dogs and monkeys had finally paid off in a—a Miracle! All those mice and dogs and monkeys had to sacrifice their ears and endure severe discomfort and intense pain in order that Jack might hear! Dr. Bangs had had to sacrifice parties, picnics with his kids, and fishing trips and Monday Night Football with his buddies in order to pick up, besides his M.D., degrees in Chemistry, Physics, Electrical and Human Engineering, Acoustics and Audiology in order that Jack might hear! Jack, say thank you! Oh, so many sacrifices had had to be made so that Jack might be given the precious gift of hearing! Jack only had to give up his natural ears (what was left of them) and his father his fortune, his mother hers, his grandparents theirs, his brothers and sisters their inheritance, the United States Government its inheritance taxes. . . . Jack, say thank you!

The rubber ears were truly a work of miracle. First, Dr. Bangs removed the dead natural ears of Jack and fashioned threaded holes in their stead where the new ears could be screwed in, or out as may be necessary for cleaning, new batteries, upgrading, or new technology. There was one little disadvantage: it was necessary to make the lobes stiffer than natural in order that the ears might be screwed in by hand. Every once in a while, they'd come a little loose and hang at funny angles, and Jack would have to screw them back in tighter, careful not to turn them too far or to tear them.

The ears worked on the principle of microwaves, emitting electronic impulses directly into the brain, bypassing the auditory nerves. They really worked! Jack could hear everything— approaching traffic, passing airplanes, music, flies buzzing, footsteps, children laughing, birds singing, the whack of bat on ball, the murmuring of a creek, the wail of his mother—everything that brings joy to the ears. Jack was thrilled. His mother was ecstatic. His father was pleased. The Director was delighted and eager to get to work on Jack's speech. This is what Oralism is all about, isn't it, she cracked, so thrilled was she to finally, at long last teach speech, really, truly, actually, bonafidically teach speech, the way speech is meant to be taught! After all, Jack can't very well be said to be deaf, I mean subhearing, anymore, can he? Get it, uh? Ha, ha, ha. Get it? Ha, ha, ha.

Everybody was happy, very happy in spite of one little quirk: Jack could hear all right, except he couldn't tell a jet overhead from a siren down the street, a robin from Drew chirping to his little fairy, a scratching on a blackboard from a squeaking hinge, and, worse, cat from bat, red from green, love from hate, boy from girl, mom from pop—all sounds sounded pretty much alike to him, almost as if all he could hear with those rubber ears was white noise.

After the first day of excitement and marvelment, Jack was disappointed. White noise isn't exactly the nicest sound in the world, you know, and it has been known to be an effective weapon of torture in certain prisons. Jack would have unscrewed the ears and thrown them away except he didn't know how he could endure people laughing at the holes in his head. It was bad enough the ears were noticeably phony, but at least no one looked his way so long as he didn't draw attention to himself.

His mother cried, "How could you be so ungrateful!?"

His father demanded of Dr. Bangs, "Why can't he understand what we say?"

"You see, it's the little hairs in the cochlea that give normal ears their marvelous ability to distinguish the fine shades of speech," the doctor explained, making a rolling gesture, now understanding why the dogs chased their tails the day long and the monkeys tried to hide their heads between their legs and howled round the clock. The rats also ran at top speed in their treadmills until they died.

Mr. Hassleback butted in, "Thought it was old men got hair in their ears . . ."

"Jack's new ears unfortunately don't have those fine hairs," the doctor went on earnestly while Mr. Hassleback paced in disgust that his joke had fallen on deaf ears. "But we're working on it, we're working on it. This is exactly the purpose of making those ears easy to replace without further surgery. Remember, your boy is the very first person on earth to have these . . ."

"Fake ears!" bellowed Mr. Hassleback.

Mrs. Hassleback cried, "Let's don't ruin this wonderful miracle!"

"Don't worry, don't worry," the Director orajected. "Everything is going to be fine; everybody is going to be very happy. Your boy will positively learn to talk! I promise!"

"How's he going to learn to talk if he can't understand nothing!?" snorted Mr. Hassleback.

"Please! Please!" pleaded Mrs. Hassleback. "We must never lose faith!"

"Okay, Okay." Mr. Hassleback threw up his hands and took out yet another mortgage on the house so the good doctor could get to work on growing real fur on a new model.

"JACK CAN hear!" Melba exulted to the class that first day of school after the summer of Jack's miracle. "Isn't it wonderful?" She applauded, encouraging with sharp nods everyone to applaud too.

All the children gathered about Jack and stared at him, or more precisely at the rubber ears. Satha reached out from behind and fingered an ear, a touch Jack never felt. "Yuck!" she yanked back her hand. He heard but did not know the source of the sound.

"Satha!" remonstrated Melba.

Tylone slipped behind Jack and ran a finger along a lobe. Wally and Casey jockeyed for their turn. Jane and Jaime got in a feel too before Melba broke them up and made them sit at their desks.

"Naughty! Naughty!" Melba scolded them. "That was not nice!"

"Jesas saw you," Jonas piped up in all earnestness.

Melba grabbed Jonas's wrist and put his palm to her cheek. "Jes-uhs," she corrected him.

"Jees-uhs."

"No, Jes-uhs."

While she was thus engaged with correcting Jonas, Tylone again sneaked behind Jack to see how far the rubber ear could be made to bend. Jack turned his head away and the ear came half-unscrewed, so that it hung horizontally.

"Ha, ha, ha," went the kids in an uproar, pointing at the funny ear and slapping their thighs.

Jack began to bawl and Melba hastened to gather him in her arms. Tears ran down her cheek as she rocked him and shot glances pregnant with reproach at brat after brat gathered about the classroom. So full of disappointment and sadness was her reproach that all the children sat down abashed.

"It's not Jack's fault he has funny ears," she said by way of teaching them the ways of tolerance, compassion, understanding, empathy, and other kindnesses. "You must understand he can't help them. God made him the way he is."

ON HIS BACK in his bed Jack wanted so much to fall off to sleep, but the white noise wailed up and down in rhythm with the arching of headlights across the ceiling. The noise jumped sharply every time David coughed. It buzzed with the snores of Wally and Jaime. It hummed as Drew responded to the little fairy in his ear. It growled with Casey fighting a dream and grunted with Tylone and yelped with Jerome. Volume and sharpness was all the white noise could convey to Jack, and he could distinguish nothing. He moaned and kicked his feet. A shriek accompanied beams of red light whipping across the ceiling.

Jack hurried to the window in time to catch a fire truck disappearing around a corner a block away. He opened the window; from the fine vantage of four stories above the corner and high above the rows and rows of two-story brownstones, he could follow the flashes of red glow upon windows and walls down the next street. He closed his eyes, hoping his rubber ears could follow the siren, but all he could hear was the white noise gradually diminishing in volume, only to be confounded by other passing traffic and David's coughing.

Nights are never total in cities, what with millions of street lamps furnishing a dirty yellow, almost umber, tinge to the air so that it, the air itself, becomes quite visible, tangible, palpable. You can actually see that it is air. The heavens above are more mud than night, and only Jupiter shows as a faint, lonely sentinel up there in the muck when the moon is out visiting elsewhere in the world. Even when the moon is up, the city does not need, does not welcome its light; you have to really look to find it. Even the huge park to the left of Jack, which from his perch four stories above the ground gives the appearance of a black hole in the midst of the city, never enjoys a true night that would make a flashlight necessary.

Jack had never known there was so much noise in the world, even so late at night. Of course, before the rubber ears, he had known there was sound all about: engines, slamming doors, bells, hearing people. His mother had told him about the noises, he had observed hearing people responding to noises, and his old hearing aid had given hints of the existence of noise, but it took the rubber ears to confirm to him that he was living in a sea of sound as much as a world of sight, and that hearing people receive images of sound as vivid as images of sight.

But the rubber ears, being synthetic, not living flesh, only gave him the sound without the image so that it was only so much noise, as featureless and meaningless as a blank white page. If only he could get something, even a crude drawing! His heart broke, as had those of the mice and dogs and monkeys in Dr. Bangs' laboratory. He made preparations to jump out the window. He didn't care if he broke his mother's heart or ruined Dr. Bangs' reputation. He was going to splatter himself on that sidewalk down there and wreck those rubber ears.

Miss Racher grabbed him just in time and dragged him back into the room and enclosed him in her tender embrace. His struggles bumped awake Tylone.

"He was gonna jump!" she cried to Tylone. He dropped his jaw, touched Jack and Miss Racher, and quickly summoned Wally, Casey, and Jaime, and they gathered about Jack now sobbing at Miss Racher's breast. She was sobbing too and rocked Jack in her arms.

He almost jump! Tylone explained, nodding at the open window. *Miss-Racher caught-him.* He ended with a gesture of plucking a hair out of his head by way of emphasizing it was a close call. Miss Racher was too astonished to remind him to use his speech. She understood every gesture clearly! She never thought she would be able to, but it seemed the gestures fit the situation so well they made perfect sense.

Jaime closed the window and the boys comforted Jack and Miss Racher with pats, hugs, and caresses, with Casey giving Miss Racher a kiss on the cheek. He thought her the loveliest person he ever saw, her hair down so that it fell upon a shoulder bare except for the strap of her nightgown, her features soft with love as she rocked Jack in her arms on her lap. In the daytime she was austere, severe, almost harsh, but now Casey thought her beautiful. He kissed her again. Her smile said thank you.

Noise, noise bother, bother me, Jack wailed. *Thought new ears help me hearie, but noise, noise bother, bother.*

Miss Racher thought she understood every gesture but glanced anxiously at Jaime for help, and he explained, "Jack said the noise bothers him. Thought the new ears would make him hearing, same as hearing people, but the noise . . ."

"Poor Jack!" Miss Racher wept again and rocked Jack.

Wish can OFF! Jack tugged at the ears. *Noise scream, scream all time!*

Jaime interpreted for Miss Racher and she agreed, "Let's see if we can turn 'em off."

They went to her room and studied the rubber ears, Jack sniffing and trying to be manly under the bright lamp and their scrutiny. *Where batteries?*

See none, Tylone frowned at the absence of little trap doors for batteries like on watches.

How? How? Jaime mused.

Jack unscrewed an ear to show how it was done, and it fell out in his hand. Even he was surprised at how easily it came off, and this made him anxious that maybe he couldn't ever get it back on again. Tiny wires connected the ear with something deep in the hole in his head, and he couldn't bring it out front far enough for a look himself.

"Let me," Jaime assured him and took the ear. The battery was now easy to see, and as tiny as a button on a dress shirt. Jaime took it out and screwed the ear back in. He did the same with the other ear and Jack beamed *Me deaf!*

Nothing wrong deaf, Casey agreed with an elaborate shrug that as much as said, what's the big deal.

Me deaf! Jack exclaimed again.

Jaime made to toss the batteries in the trashcan, but Miss Racher said, "Let me have 'em. I'll think of a way to make 'em dead and put 'em back in. Nobody will know."

Secret! Exulted, the boys and Miss Racher swore to each other to keep the secret always.

Jack was very happy to be an object of a dangerous secret and to be deaf, finally. Deaf at long last! His relief was evident and Miss Racher did not require much persuasion to let him go back to bed alone. He slept well that night and every night thereafter.

Pamela Wright-Meinhardt

PAMELA WRIGHT-MEINHARDT graduated from Gallaudet University in 1998, and now resides in Arizona. She is proud of her job as a middle school English teacher, where she hopefully is creating future writers! She has lived in Alabama, Florida, Montana, and Washington, D.C., and living in different places has given her opportunities to meet a wide variety of people and have unique experiences. She also has spent several years in theater and doing art. Wright-Meinhardt includes all these experiences in her writing, drawing from what she has seen and heard. She has been writing since she was a pre-teen and has won several awards and competitions through the years. She currently spends time with her family, and she continues to write, help out at the local theater, and expand her knowledge.

When They Tell Me . . .

Montana: April 23, 2001

When they tell me
    That my thoughts cannot possibly be powerful
    Because my voice cannot create beauty
I feel angry.
But I am not allowed anger
For to be angry is to be defiant.

When they tell me
    That to be good I must be obedient, taciturn, never cause trouble
    To comply gratefully in the face of insults and humiliation
I feel rage.
But I am not allowed rage
For to feel rage is to be a radical.

When they tell me
    I should shamefully shun the fluency that flows from my hands
    And erase the grotesque emotions and information from my face
I feel revulsion.
But I am not allowed revulsion
For to feel revulsion is to be a disgrace.

When they tell me
    I should pretend to happily conform
    And find satisfaction from a part-time life on the fringe
I feel despair.
But I am not allowed despair
For to feel despair is to be unappreciative.

When they tell me
    That my life of silence has no value, no significance, and no sense
    For easing the way for those too young to know
I feel hate.
But I am not allowed hate
For to feel hate is to be a militant.

When they tell me
    I don't realize how deprived I am, how isolated and behind
    And that my people cannot ever succeed without someone holding
    their hand
I feel aghast.
But I am not allowed aghast
For to feel aghast is to refuse to assimilate.

When they tell me
    I cannot be tenacious, I must accept coercion;
    I cannot be opinionated, I must accept debasement;
    I cannot be intense, I must accept degradation;
    I cannot be confident, I must accept abuse;
    I cannot aspire, I must accept inferiority;
    I am not allowed resentment, I'd be a troublemaker;
    I am not allowed fury, I'd be a rebel;
    I am not allowed horror, I'd be abnormal;
    I am not allowed frustration, I'd be insane;
And if I dare . . .
I'd be diseased.

How dare I?
Oh, do I dare!
I do dare!
    And I can!
But I am not allowed strength
For I am not allowed to be human.

Silent Howl

I have seen the best souls of my world sodomized by a scheming uniform system and left to struggle, vegetating, for a breath of life.

I have seen intense camadaries distorted and suppressed by a narrow, one-way, uncompromising larder of a society; determined cohesions crammed into incredible parodies and puppeteeringly masqueraded.

I have seen multitudes of children left alone in classrooms, misplaced and ignored, moved through grades and coddled, spoonfed, then kicked out into the cesspool of an incomprehensible reality tyrannically totalitarianed by those who can hear, and

I have seen the same darkness follow the same children home to loneliness and television, television, television, eating dinner in a closed little sphere and disappearing to bed unnoticed because Mommy and Daddy are too disinterested to try.

I have seen my language annihilated, mocked, shunned, belittled, doubted, analyzed, scientified, and butchered by know-it-alls who arrogantly believe their robotic hands emulate the natural unconscious grace of those who've internalized its fluency.

I have seen the beauty that flows from my hands researched, and researched, proved again and again to be valid then shoved into a clinical paragraph and skeptically disputed for scores of years.

I have seen pride hooked onto machines, machinated and cyborgic, programmed to repeatedly utter sounds difficult to decipher and shoved into grotesquely embarrassing, undignified positions; all for an experiment on his voice.

I have seen Kleenex, wooden tongue depressors, mirrors and fingers become tools of torture and writhing shame as condescending speech pathologists quote obscure success stories and wield a godly fist over unsuspecting and trusting frightened kids crunching themselves into the creases of their chairs.

I have seen children being told for years that their speech was ideal and beautiful then publicly humiliated by giggling perplexed teenagers ringing up the cash registers.

I have seen babies born into excited acceptance, proudly cherished and adulated in a world where voice finds little value then forcibly convinced by those governed by fears that silence is *not* golden but a festering deviance; confusedly growing up into degrading categorizations.

I have seen barely toddling babies' heads experimentally opened up and sliced and drilled then fitted with electrodes, magnets, wires and machines for a life of electrical-cords-coming-out-of-my-head existence to pacify ashamed, scared, unrelenting parents.

I have seen righteous teachers employ a vise of control over crying, frightened, and begging-for-mercy kindergartners making them Show-and-Tell, Show-and-Tell their hearing apparatuses to each and every curious pair of eyes in the classroom; teaching the longstanding mandated "different is wrong."

I have seen dull-eyed parents blankly with hands folded humbly turn to the college-degreed experts, placing their child unresistingly into the ready-to-rescue hands of those tunnelvisioning towards "normalcy."

I have seen the baccalaureated, mastered, and doctor-of-philosophied deaf deeply teeth their lips, fixate a stare on table cracks, press the blood out of their hands while watching protocol take control, another child corralled into the Can't-Be-Me mentality.

I have seen high schoolers sent to face crowds battling peer-pressured acceptance while self-consciously toting obnoxiously bulky headpieces with antennae, boxes with wires, buttons and lights beepingly announcing loudly all the fix-it hopes and standardizationing decrees.

I have seen teenagers fightingly overcompensate, grossly loading on more and more tasks while their parents heartily cheer on the futile battle, both believing somehow, in some way, perhaps there may be a transformation into someone who can fool them all.

I have seen again and again celebration granted to the pretenders shedding the soaringly blessed difference that empowers, but chooses to hobble weighted down by guilt on the ground blending into millions.

I have seen limelight-loving, praise-seeking, far-from-qualified, barely signing interpreters become daytime mothers, a gossiping friend, walking cheat-sheets, a classroom buddy sticking up in a fight, the mouth, the brain and the life of a solitary but least restrictively appropriately mainstreamed, inclusioned and "so-called-very-close-to-normal" child.

I have seen paternalists reach out hands and hearts to those in dire need, spartanly donating precious time, energy and focus, pastorly citing the benefits of giving without getting, then turn away with fear, complete puzzlement, confused anger and incredulous awe from one of us standing, clear-eyed, well versed, and without need.

I have seen a those-who-can-hear continuum from high school dropouts to university professors firmly believe Aristotelian claims that all of us are in all cases incapable of thought or reason, then wondered as

I have seen rights-fighting groups from all walks terrorize with fear, making people stammer, intimidated, hurriedly searching for a stable, inoffensive, unmistakingable string of words, and I have enviously desired some of that power while

I saw the same cowering, chattering crowd transform Hydelike into holier-than-thous, turning to spit biting, disapproving glances at our dramatic expressiveness; the beauty they perceive as freaky animation, our massive expanse of poetic body cinematics.

I have seen hordes of religion-guided do-gooders from all denominations chase down the poor little deaf souls needing to be put on a platter and brought to Jesus, and when an elusive one is caught,

I have seen their looks of smug satisfaction and self-laudation for so brilliantly conquering one of the lost, dark, unexposed, and oh so isolated.

I have seen fresh-faced boys and pig-tailed girls wide-eyedly broadcasted, televised before congregations of hundreds and slapped to be cured by babbling pretentious fraudulent fanatics for desperate parents' attempts at the perfect.

I have seen officers of the law handcuff innocents, raping their communication and jeeringly throw them into penned units without the Miranda and held without word or a phone call for hours, or days, and

I have seen ambulance speed to hospitals with good intentions and the nervous doctors' dismissal without tested explanations, then those ER visits followed by hearses with the dishonored luckless riding forever solemn, and

I have seen universities deny intelligent, frequently well-proven abilities a continuing education, some going as far as to alter success to falsify a failure, and

I have seen employers abruptly fire good, diligent, devoted workers in need of little upgrading and

I have seen young children forced by judges to hear and speak for their parents for bankruptcies, for divorces, for criminalities, for this and for that and for God knows what else in front of menageried courtrooms, and

I have seen bankers talk loans, doctors talk cancer, dentists talk pain, cashiers talk change, teachers talk progress, and day after day of others use the same child to talk, and

I have seen all of these smilingly excused by "Oh, sorry. An interpreter wasn't in the budget."

I have seen erroneous medicines prescribed on fantastical assumptions passing as diagnoses and further sickness result, many close to death calls.

I have seen those wrongly accused and misexamined, those without the self-protection of language thrown into mental institutions and filed away for decades.

I have seen the young and ambitious fill out scores of applications seeking employment, entrusting faith in new empowering laws, only to be again coldly and regardlessly told, "We don't take your kind."

I have seen nonlethal genocide, the cognitively murdered, a withering, despairing generation of do we have any choices surrenderingly fading lost into the foggy smoke of alcoholcocaineheroinmarijuanamethamphetamines.

I have seen mothers ununderstandingly tricked by the well-intended (such as their own parents) into signing papers legal and binding, unknowingly releasing custody of their children, then sent home in wonderment only to realize days later, heartwreckingly, that they have been rendered childless, vehemently unwilling and with despair must face life without their babies.

I have seen self-servers ride the coattails of their prized model darling's oh-so-delightfully-normal successes, spouting hard-luck stories, profiting fame and fortune off the bridges burned, door shut and confusion beaten amok for many others searching for direction.

I have seen looks of pity and uncomfortable grins, openmouthed stares, twisted expressions, and shunning eyes, all towards an unpleasant disquiet and chuckling anxiety; a discomfort not at all my own.

I have seen tearstained years of speech-training succeed (hallelujah!), to follow with teeth grinding years of learning one must perpetually, constantly, silently, quietly be unmilitantly docile.

I have seen strong-willed individuals crumble in desperation, flailing in frustration, crying out in a fight against helplessness, and straining against steely chains, clinging to stubbornly optimistic desires against constant oppression and ignorance, and

I have seen denials repeatedly Uncle Tom-ed, the wishfully daring becoming fodder for pinching, parroting crabs retrogressingly destroying courage with silence, but

I have seen a degree of intensity unparalleled and lovely, and explosion of unity and tenacious respect; quick perseverance and worldwide pride; an ironclad embrace on a way of life; a passionate loyalty, unmatched, unequalled, unwavering, and loved.

A Letter to C. F.

IF YOU ASK a ballerina, a watercolorist, a violinist, a writer, an actor on the stage, or any other artist where their craft comes from, they will often tell you they are just another medium for Art, on the same level as the paintbrush, pen or bow. Art swells up inside of them, in waves of crescendos and silences until bursting forth on the canvas with which they have been gifted.

In short, Art starts in the heart and is meant to touch hearts.

It is folly to think, then, that not being able to hear prevents a person from being inspired by sounds. The organ of the ear is a small compartment of a whole, not the whole of a person. Millions of nerves race through a body; what's to say a few in the ear destroy a person's ability to understand music? Or poetry? Or simply to have their hearts touched? And if the message is acoustic, is it always missed? Absolutely not.

It is also absurd to say that being able to hear is always a blessing, and not being able to hear is not. God's blessings come in many forms, and it would be sacrilegious to judge the forms in which these blessings come. One who cannot hear could easily be blessed more so than his hearing counterpart. According to Keats:
"Heard melodies are sweet, but those unheard
Are sweeter; therefore, ye soft pipes, play on;

I took a Shakespeare class one semester. On the first day, the professor, a grizzly old man who had been teaching at the university level since he was 23, announced to the class that he pitied deaf people. In his lecture, he explained that deaf people missed so much of the beauty of language, especially the spoken magic of the dramatic voice. I calmly sat through class and then wrote him a letter in response. C. F. and I eventually reached a level of sincere and mutual respect.

Not to the sensual ear, but, more endeared
Pipe to the spirit ditties of no tone:"

A person who cannot hear can easily have a lifelong love affair with words. They can sigh to Byron's languid sensuality or Whitman's a nerve-jarring barbaric yawps, to Ginsberg's howling staccato, or the lyrical swinging of Ferlinghetti's perpetual wait for wonder. They can internalize the passions of the gods and complexities of human nature constrained into a single line of Shakespeare. They can, if they choose, move away from the canon of literature. They can have a hundred million miracles! With a little bit of luck they can have their Jellicle hearts climb every mountain, dance all night at the ballet, in their corner of the sky with Rodgers and Hammerstein, or Lerner and Loewe! Oh, not to forget Andrew Lloyd Webber, or Stephen Schwartz, and many others! S'wonderful, s'marvelous, isn't it? How do they do it? Fools give you reasons, but wise men never try.

But what about music? What about the tinkling of a harp, the whine of a flute, the rolling of a cello, or the three-dimensionality of a symphony? Music, though elusive to those who cannot hear, can be loved. This love can run into anguishing depths, much like Galileo loving his distant and mysterious stars. For one who cannot hear, music becomes a persistent child, inching his way into a life until the soul cannot exist without him.

Granted, there are times that not being able to hear is a sadness indeed; and beauty passes by unaware. However, it is sadder that in this life there are many who hear but do not listen, those who look but do not see, and those hearts that contain vast potential for love and brotherhood, but remain closed and brittle with cold or hatred. Is lack of hearing then a handicap if one who cannot hear can listen, feel, understand, and love?

Some of us who cannot hear have the gift, or curse, bestowed upon us by God and Fate. . . . This is the ability to understand sounds, music, and poetry without actually hearing them. We embrace this anomaly, this strangeness inside of ourselves. It swells inside us, in crescendos and silences, takes a life of its own, and without it, we cannot exist. And we would not choose any other way to be.

Kristi Merriweather

KRISTI MERRIWEATHER is a young African-American Deaf woman. She is a student and lives in Greenbelt, Maryland.

Be Tellin' Me

People tell me
what they think
a black deaf female is
People tell me
what they think
they know
what a black deaf female is
People tell me
they know the deal
behind all deals
just a simple solution
mix in the deaf culture,
add an equal amount of
black culture,
stir well and smoothly,
pronto, the black deaf culture,
I say
excuse my standard English, but
f _ _ _ you
I don't take no
second-handed,
mulatto,
prescribed,
whittled-down,
semi-that,
half-here,
part-this
culture,
uh-huh,

I be cookin' up my own recipe,
spicy, like mama taught me,
no, don't need your bowl,
thank you very much,
only I be
tellin' me
what a blakdeafemale is.

Remember

Out of Motherland Africa, ripped from my people
into the iron-heavy chains, stifling my motions,
I look at the sea, the dark threatening waters awaiting
to carry us on an endless, wicked journey,
    I heard my weeping mother yell to me,
        "Remember."

Out of slavery, Lord knows the scars and horrors my
hands, body, mind, & soul been through,
I've forgotten my language, my home, my hopes, my
culture, or even where my family are,
Yet, as I watch my people heading for the cities of North
or the farms of South,
no money, no food, no clear guidance,
    Somewhere I heard my mother whisper to me,
        "Remember."

Out of Jim Crow, with all its burning crosses and
burnt promises,
facing the stony faces of those that wear the badge of
law and order, holding the nightsticks that have
senselessly beat thousands of my people while we sang
"We shall overcome" and trying to keep believing that,
Raise your Black Power fist
Say Right on, Black is beautiful,
Don't know why my head is hurting, some kind of image
is trying to fight its way into it,
    It's screaming my mother's voice and eyes saying,
        "Remember."

Out of the burning riots of LA,
Through the red smoke of anger finally unleashed,
I stand motionless to see the images finally flashing
Before my eyes,
The drug dealers gaining control,
The bullets flying toward our people by our own brothers,
The punch of the rap lyrics attacking the dignity of sisters,
Poverty, unwanted pregnancies, AIDS, clarence and anita
Suddenly I saw the image of my mother signing to me,
    "Remember."

It Was His Movin' Hands

Know what I mean,
don't you just know that feeling of
that thing white folks call
electricity sparking
that think black folks like us call
good vibes
that gets that funky eyeplay started
our smiles manifesting,
rebelling
against our wishes
to appear
kool,
breezy kind of c-oo-ool, superfly
yeah, like that,
magick kickin' in,
sirens a-blarin'
peripheral vision gone malfunctioning
shoot,
it's obvious
we're losin' the control game,
shamelessly,
breakin' the rules,
ah, but
what's deafsista like me
gonna do, gonna do
with her mind shootin' up
into Milky Way, outta my reach.

Raymond Luczak

RAYMOND LUCZAK is the author of *St. Michael's Fall: Poems* (Deaf Life Press), *Silence Is a Four-Letter Word: On Art & Deafness*, and *This Way to the Acorns: Poems* (both from The Tactile Mind Press); he also edited *Eyes of Desire: A Deaf Gay and Lesbian Reader* (Alyson). A playwright and screenwriter, Luczak lives in New York, where he is completing his debut feature film, *Ghosted*, which he produced and directed. His URL is www.raymondluczak.com.

How to Become a Backstabber

1. Discover the Value of Your Own Deafness.

This is not as easy as it sounds. If you are deaf, many people—including some deaf people themselves—think that you shouldn't limit yourself by solely communicating through signs, and that if you have sufficient hearing, you should use speech whenever possible. This depends on your background, of course. You, for example, were born hearing, but you lost most of your hearing at the age of four due to rubella. You are the second daughter, and the only deaf person, in your family.

You have been told that sign language is bad, so you watched your hands carefully. Vigilance became one of your stalwart qualities as you sat and mostly daydreamed through mainstreamed classes, and spoke. You enjoyed speech lessons immensely because it meant getting attention. You didn't mind the repetitive drills of consonants and vowels, and the pronunciation of words you'd never heard before.

One day, though, your life was forever changed. You meet Billy, a *second* deaf student, who was actually hard-of-hearing but had spent most of his education in a deaf school recently closed by the state, and who uses sign language. You are fascinated in spite of your speech therapist's constant admonitions; you feel funny when she tries to force Billy's signing hands down on the table. You look at your own hands, wondering.

Those high school days were wonderful because of the clandestine language. You have mixed feelings when your hearing classmates come up to you and say, "Marlee Matlin's so amazing," or "Heather Whitestone's inspiring." You don't dare admit that you can't understand Matlin's signing at all, or that you feel funny about Whitestone's implied opinion of oralism being far superior to sign language. You are constantly badgered by hearing classmates on whether you know the sign for this or that, and your opinions on this or that deaf person in the media, but you don't dare come out of the closet. You have nightmares in which your hands are chopped off and your tongue is anointed with holy speech.

Your speech therapist asks you daily whether you've learned any signs from Billy. You shake your head no. Everyone you know adores your speech, but Billy much prefers your hands. Everything is so easy, *easy* to say with hands, and *easy* to tell on your hands whether the signs are clearly enunciated—the inestimable beauty of hearing with one's eyes.

2. Spend a Great Deal of Time With Your Deaf Friends.

In a hearing college two hundred miles away from home, you hook up with some deaf students. You discover a world of language, culture, and friendship. High school is a dim memory, and you no longer remember why you'd once had such a huge crush on this or that hearing boy. Billy, your first deaf friend, is now at Gallaudet University. You can't imagine going away to a school hundreds and hundreds of miles away, and going there without even checking it out first. But that's what he did. He had been so unhappy with all those hearing classmates in high school, and he'd wanted to quit and find any old job anywhere. You are still relieved that he stuck it out, and that he actually sent you a postcard from Gallaudet, as promised. He wrote, NO MORE HEARIES. HAPPY HAPPY <u>HAPPY</u>!!!

In your dorm room you stare at the postcard for a long time and tack it on the bulletin board above your desk. Happy? Him happy? It is hard to imagine him that way, really. He was always so pissed off at the world, especially at the state legislators who decided his deaf school wasn't worth the expense and shut it down for good. The state's debts compounded by a limp economy, had grown too large to ignore. You vow to visit Gallaudet one day.

Your deaf friends at college tell you stories from their lives, and you begin to feel warmly whole. At home you still speak, and you don't tell your parents that you're using American Sign Language out in the open at school. You are eternally grateful that they're paying your tuition, but you know they'll never understand you as you are. The very idea of you using ASL would break their hearts. After all, they've donated a great deal of money to the Alexander Graham Bell Association over the years, and are often listed prominently in *The Volta Review*.

Yet their love for you can't be mistaken for paternalism. They've genuinely tried to encourage you to participate in various extra-curricular activities at school, and they do attend as your devoted cheerleaders. You love them because no one else cheered for you when you came in next-to-last in women's track, or when your science project won third place. You were never told that you couldn't achieve anything because you were deaf. But the unspoken corollary was that sign language would hinder you in insidious ways.

But those stories told by your deaf friends enrage you. They were unjustly punished merely for wanting to communicate, even if it meant through their hands. You vow never to let that happen again, and you take out your AGB membership card and light it with a friend's match. They clap with glee, and you know you've found a better home than your parents could possibly imagine for you.

3. Ignore the Little Insecurities That Nag at Your Deaf Pride.

After graduation, you move to Seattle. You find a job as a computer technician; you had been surprised by how much fun it was to fix those damn things in college, and now you can't believe that you actually get *paid* to do such things. Of course, the fact that you are both female and deaf seems to bother some of your clients, but they say nothing when they observe your troubleshooting speed. Boom-boom-*boom*. You're out the door, and your clients are already raving about you to their friends.

You still talk with your parents through e-mail.

In time, you meet a cute deaf man named George. You fall for him because of the way he signs, in a slowpokey kind of way. He is a computer programmer, but he is such a child at heart. He plays games all the time, he thinks nothing of wrestling with buddies in the living room, and he has a big heart. He comes from a deaf-strong family, and you are struck by how included you feel in his family. They welcome you with open arms, they are so relieved to see that you're indeed deaf. Just like them. They don't have to justify their ways to you. You and George become engaged.

When your parents meet George for the first time, they turn quiet with rage. They don't say anything about his gravelly voice or bad speech, but they are not forthcoming with hugs or attempts to be close, as they were with your hearing sister's boy-friend—now her husband. That day, out of eyeshot, George turns to you and says, "Hearing control wedding don't-want."

You compromise with two weddings, the first one taking place in a deaf church. On the day that you marry, your parents weep, unable to communicate with those who clearly care for you, as a deaf person who has embraced them; your sister keeps smiling as if nothing is wrong. You send interpreters their way, but they're too frightened to make conversation with anyone. They can't stop watching how George and his pals carry on as if they never left school; in fact, you envy their shared past and their tight-knittedness. Your parents cannot disguise their discomfort, even with your second wedding in their church where you always sat in the third row to be able to lipread the minister.

With your husband, you find yourself more and more drawn into the deaf community. He reminds you not to pay any attention to the gossip swirling around you: Dave makes nearly twice what you make, and he's only two years out of college! You *saw* his paycheck. Mina has married a hearing man who can't sign shit, and she comes from a deaf-strong family! Scott, a heavy-set oralist, brings his hearing thin lover to a particularly rowdy night at the deaf bowling club! The guy has a tan so dark that his peroxided hair looks white. You *saw* him carrying on like a sissy in front of all those beer-toting straight bowlers. And worse yet, that bitch who stole your best friend's husband now claims to have known your boss all her life! You *saw* him nodding and smiling anxiously around her.

George reminds you not to pay attention to all of this.

You repeat the grumbly things he has said about this or that pal of his.

He rolls his eyes, as if to say, "They're just *deaf*, okay?"

But it is not long before you serve gossip along with toast in the morning, constantly comparing yourselves with these people.

4. Spend So Much Time With Your Deaf Friends That You Practically *Have* to Start Talking About Each Other. (A corollary: The Smaller the Community, the Better.)

With the birth of your first baby, you suddenly feel the overwhelming presence of deaf in-laws peeking out of the shadows, wondering whether your Eileen is hearing or not. Six months later she is found to be deaf, and there is so much jubilation on George's face that he breaks into tears. You decide to stay home for a year or two, then longer when you learn of your second pregnancy. Your next baby, Robert, is hearing. You put your job on hold.

With both children you never use your voice. You simply sign, almost forcibly teaching your children *signs* instead of speech. Their eyes light up when they see you signing to them. They can't stop grasping for your fingers. You are so full of love, so full of hugs for them at every turn, that even George has to chuckle. You two no longer talk about other people, but about what's best for your beautiful, *beautiful* babies. At home, you feel at peace, more so when George in his boxer shorts twaddles around with the children trying to climb up the moving mountain of their father in the living room.

Sometimes some of your deaf friends who are also mothers visit with their kids, which is always great. Naturally, everyone talks babies, but you suddenly feel a little out of it when they start discussing Al, one of your husband's best pals. Seems that he's been having an affair with a deaf high school senior girl, and his wife, Betty, hasn't talked to him ever since she found out.

You don't know Al very well, even though he's the one who's always there whenever George needs help with moving huge furniture around, or building the back porch, or painting all the walls upstairs in your new house. You've never sat down and talked with him as a person, not as someone who's known your husband all his life. You like him, though, because he is clearly a good man, a citadel of reliability, and someone *seeming* incapable of dishonesty. Before you'd heard all of this about Al, you wouldn't have used the word "seeming." Everyone, you thought, really liked him.

You bring up the story with George later that night.

"What tell you before?" He explodes. "Not true! Not true!"

Nevertheless, you vow to keep an eye peeled for any telling detail.

5. Pretend to be Concerned in Front of the People Involved.

At a social party held for local alumni from the National Technical Institute of the Deaf—your husband George had earned his bachelor's in Computer Science there through the Rochester Institute of Technology—you run into Al's wife. You are pleasantly surprised to find that she doesn't seem embittered at all. Betty comes up to you and asks how you are doing.

You share the latest on your babies. Eileen is now walking and climbing like crazy, and has to be fenced in no matter what. Robert is obsessed with eating asparagus, dipped in mayonnaise. Betty laughs at the image of your boy dipping and flipping the mayo all over the kitchen floor before eating the stalk.

Finally, you broach the subject. "How you?"

She doesn't let on whether she knows that you probably know. "Fine A-L work tonight." Of course. He works the graveyard shift at a Microsoft factory, keeping an eye on its security. It's a tough job because so many packages slip out in the back and end up getting sold on the streets of New York and elsewhere way below wholesale, and the guards often get the heat for it. You remember how Al had explained all of this to you one night, when you were all a great crowd who always got together every weekend to party. That was a long time before any babies were born.

She smiles and says nothing more.

You glance around the room, full of people whose faces you know, and most of whom you've gotten acquainted with here and there through various deaf social functions over the years. You turn to Betty. "Me sorry."

Her face turns a little hard. "Gossip stupid."

"Betty. Stories true?"

"Play dumb you? Good."

"Me-not-say-that."

A mutual friend enters the room with her husband, and Betty is gone, waving hello. You turn and catch Michelle's knowing glance; she's married to one of George's pals. Seems you weren't the first to ask Betty tonight.

6. Instead of Feeling Hurt, Wear Your Feelings On The Outside.

For days afterwards you can't stop wondering whether your trustworthiness has become devalued among your friends, and whether they've been talking badly about you. You've been in the deaf community long enough to see how some deafies can easily spread inaccurate and hurtful stories, if only to destroy the ones they don't like. Often, when you and George talk about throwing a party at your house, you two have to write down the list of all the guests and see if you know of any bad blood among any of them. Sometimes it gets too complicated, and the party almost always never happens any more.

One day, some friends come over for coffee and bring their kids. Once they're satisfied that their kids are indeed safe in your child-proofed backyard, they share the latest soap opera installments on this or that deaf person you all know either by sight or by acquaintance. Somehow, without thinking, you pry loose some deep-down opinions. George's always warned you of sharing your innermost thoughts with people you think are friends, but these days he seems constantly weary; at his company, the project of migrating from Windows 95 to a whole new—and invariably better—operating system has become much bigger than anticipated, what with bugs in the hardware and politics within George's department. Completely attentive, the friends are suddenly yours. Their appetite for what you think of others seems insatiable. They nod agreement, and when it's time for them to leave, you know you've hit on something. You're not sure what it is, but you like the sensation of feeling this intense kinship with them.

7. Warning: Someone Will Backstab You Sooner or Later. (Usually Sooner.)

You are buckling the kids into their special seats in the back of the car when you catch George giving a slight wave to a beautiful blonde strutting by to the supermarket behind you. You know he didn't think you'd catch that, but you have sharp eyes. Ever since these friends keep coming back for your thoughts, you've become much more aware of how men behave among themselves and among women not their wives.

You sit down in the car. "Saw you."

"Me do-do?"

"Girl over-there you wave."

"Looked-at-me smile."

"Smile finish wrong?"

He turns the ignition key and says nothing.

When you are all home, and the food has been put away, he turns to you. "Heard many-many stories about you. Friends some-them don't-want visit come over any more. Sick-you gossip."

Usually the loquacious one, you feel unable to say anything.

8. Above all, deny that you've ever said a bad word or spread rumors about anyone.

That night you snuggle up to George's back. You lick his sweet back slowly, in the way he'd said turned him on, but tonight he doesn't respond. You know you've lost something, something that these friends of yours wouldn't understand. You sigh, thinking instead about your kids, and how much they need a father in today's darkening world.

In time, he will probably have affairs with other women, who usually outnumber deaf men by a wide margin; no wonder that deaf wives can be extremely jealous of single deaf women. In time, George will extend more of his love on your kids; of course, he still loves you and talks with you and all that, but it's not the same. And in time, some of his pals will return to watch sports on his huge TV, if only because they missed his company. But you'll always be remembered as someone who'd neglected the vigilance of watching her own hands.

Depths of the River

ALL HER LIFE Angie had heard in whispers, always half-believing, half-doubting, about the river people. No one ever saw them out of the water, but many who lived on the banks of the snaking Abbott River sensed the very distinctive presence of intelligent creatures who didn't just swim around like fish, but nonetheless lived just under the surface. No one could describe their facial features precisely, but no one could forget their eyes, the way they blinked slowly with their translucent eyelids as they stared upward from underwater. Needless to say, this creepiness scared away parents who'd wanted to buy houses with a backyard river for their children. Many factories further upstream folded soon after dumping toxic wastes, even illegally in the guise of night. Factory workers were too spooked by disembodied sounds of pain and yearning, and left in hordes after reliving inarticulate nightmares of water and sound.

The towns lining the recalcitrant river knew enough not to rely on it for anything; it was a presence that tourists and visitors did not quite comprehend—they only sensed its sinister power. So it was hardly surprising that so many towns, once booming a century ago, dwindled. No one could pinpoint when the river acquired its incontestable power; even the local historical societies couldn't find any mention of the river's strange character after combing through the diaries of those who founded their towns on the river.

Long ago, when Angie was twenty-seven, she turned to prostitution when she lost everything: her job, her husband, her children, her home. Her short temper had lost her job as receptionist in a town that had no other openings left; her desperately clinging loneliness and philandering husband ended her miserable marriage; her fists battered her constantly-crying babies, and they eventually had to be handed over to her self-righteous sister; and her inability to meet her mortgage payments after her husband left her meant the end of her home. All this happened many years ago, all acknowledged with slowly shaking heads by ladies who gathered for cups of coffee after weekday masses at Our Lady of the Rosary whenever Angie strolled by in a mini-skirt and a waist-high mink coat in the cold of winter. Later, when she finally lost her looks to age, she built herself a small shack deep inside the woods on the fringes of Joe Peabody's river property. There, Angie installed a small wood stove, a bed, and a trunkload of blankets. She had no friends, for she was left with what any aging prosti-tute in a small town had: a bad reputation and a thorough lack of interest in her as a person. She sat for hours next to the puffy stove, feeling the crisp heat caress her face while she dreamed of love, the kind that existed only in pulp romances.

One morning, when the old woman leaned over to scoop up the ice-cold water from the Abbott River with her bucket, she saw a baby floating in his bassinet. As it floated slowly by, the baby never once made a sound, just slept contentedly as if there was nothing to fuss about. She leaped into the river, which she'd never done all her life, as she'd always been afraid of the river people she sensed lived nearby, and caught the bassinet before it could pass. Angie pulled it along to the shore and brought it into her warm shack. There, as Angie dried herself, she kept staring at the baby. It was slightly strange-looking; it looked like a baby, yet there was a transparent aura of old age and jaundice surrounding it.

An hour later, she brought the baby over to Joe Peabody's house; from there, she became front page news in the local news-papers. The police searched the birth records of all the hospitals within a thirty-mile radius, even going so far as to query the one-hundred-and-three doctors to see if they could account for the births of their recently pregnant patients. Nothing. Every recent birth and pregnancy in the area was accounted for. It was a bizarre case because the blankets keeping the baby warm were hardly wet, which meant someone had carefully sent his bassinet off from upstream perhaps ten to twenty minutes before.

No one knew what more could be done with the baby, other than feeding it and keeping it warm. The fact that Angie used her shack as her "address" enabled her to collect her monthly welfare checks; she did not spend much, but saved instead for a rainy day. The savings would now go toward the baby, nicknamed Moses after the baby who was found floating along the Nile River in the Bible. Angie was not well-liked, but no one else seemed to want a baby of unknown parentage; and there was something freakish, slightly unhuman, about the baby.

When the social services office first learned that the old woman was taking the baby after all, they visited her shack twice, sometimes three times, a day. They demanded that she move out of her substandard housing into a better government-subsidized apartment on the other side of town, a far distance away from the river she so feared and loved. She did not argue, paying close attention to any need that Moses might have, and taking extra good care of him. The unconditional love she displayed, whether the social service workers were observing her or not, was truly moving, and soon the workers maneuvered through the red tape to give her a bigger monthly check. Still, Angie continued to save a little bit every month.

Each day the old woman performed the same routine without fail: change diapers, sterilize the bottle before feeding, give the baby a warm bath, and toss a few bright toys above him before he turned his head to sleep. An hour or so later, she would check his diaper to see whether it was soiled, and change accordingly. She sometimes cooed lullabies to him as she bottle-fed him in a rocking chair donated to her by the local St. Vincent de Paul's thrift shop. Never having felt so appreciated, or so respected after years of being called the one-time town whore, she had never felt happier, or more delighted with the joy of being needed.

A year soon passed in this way.

On the anniversary of finding the baby bubbling by her old shack, Angie noticed again that Moses had not gained much weight, yet he seemed much older with his weary eyes; he never outgrew his baby clothes. Of course, the fact that he never made a sound hadn't bothered her in the beginning, as he was such a good baby who slept well through the night. But he wasn't making a single sound; just flickers of emotion on his face whenever he saw something.

One of the social workers noticed this and suggested that he go in for a hearing test.

He was found to have absolutely no residual hearing. Hearing aids or cochlear implants would be useless. She wondered out loud about the sign language she'd have to learn. The social workers admonished her gently, saying that there was a more immediate problem, and that was his lack of physical growth. Some said that he might turn out to be a dwarf, or maybe a midget. Geneticists were brought in to examine the baby's DNA, but the tests conducted proved to be inconclusive. They needed to see his parents' chromosomes to be more definite.

There was nothing really to do but to pray for the baby's parents to show up.

As the following year passed, the old woman gestured to this or that object in the apartment and in the playground behind the complex while she used her voice. Moses responded emphatically with a gleeful pointing back to the old woman or to the swing or to a group of children playing in the sandbox. But still the baby did not grow an inch or gain a pound, and he didn't even try to crawl or stand or walk.

In time, the baby reached approximately three years of age. He remained the same weight he was the day she found him. Even though she never told anyone, she was deeply worried: Would people think she was being a bad mother? His doctor said that the baby exhibited no dehydration or respiratory or immune system problems; perhaps Moses was mentally retarded. But the subsequent brain scans showed that the baby's electromagnetic waves were absolutely normal.

Angie fretted and fretted and fretted. Was this God's way of punishing her for all her past sins by giving her a bundle of joy who'd never grow up? The baby was physically alive, but spiritually dead. Truly, it couldn't be her fault if he didn't respond to even the most nutritiously-balanced meal plans she followed right to the teaspoon.

One day she asked her neighbor to give her a ride downtown and drop her off near the park where the Abbott River flowed past the picnicking area. She pushed the bassinet on its wheels to the river's edge and looked both ways. This being a weekday, and in the middle of September, no one was around. She lifted the baby and bassinet off its wheels and waded through the shallow waters, stopping short of the powerful undercurrents lurking beneath the cascading surface.

Then she closed her eyes, let go, and saw a most amazing sight.

The bassinet splintered instantly into a dozen pieces, but the baby did not go under. Instead, the baby was using his arms as if he'd always known the river, all his limbs, paddling furiously, and his body slowly elongated until it become the body of a young man's. Moses did not waver from the spot where she had let go; he was a whirlpool by himself. The young man did not seem to see her as he dove, naked as a dolphin, deeper into the river and far away.

She stood watching, shivering from the chilly waters gripping her body.

As she plowed her way back to the shore, she began to sense a strange movement around her feet. She paused, watching the waves rolling around her calves, and saw a pair of translucently human eyes staring up at her. The eyes were his, and they were no longer weary or old; he was completely alive, vivid.

She watched him in the clear water as he turned to a woman who was clearly his mother. She seemed to be trying to explain something with her hands, but he seized her by the throat in a rage. Angie sensed that the mother had sent him off in a bassinet to die. She stood transfixed as his mother's body evaporated into a puddle of particles that diffused downstream.

She took the long way home and sat so contentedly, lost in the sadness of his absence yet overjoyed to know that Moses was indeed happy at last, that it was a few days before one of the social workers thought to check up on her.

No one believed the old woman's tale. In fact, people threatened to put her in jail for murdering the baby and burying it somewhere in parts unknown. But the police had searched every inch of Joe Peabody's woods and found none. Nor could anyone could find the dead body of his mother—if that was his mother—in the river.

The judge felt pity for her as Angie was close to eighty years old. He dismissed her case for lack of evidence. She hadn't hurt anyone at all. Listless, she gave the money away to everyone she knew on the street, even paying back some of her regular customers from the years they'd frequented her, and she moved back to the old shack. She died a few mornings later, during the first frost of autumn. Moses looked all around before stepping out of the river to carry her dead body deep into their water, where she fell into the most shimmery whirlpool of arms, found herself breathing a watery youth with a pair of hands throbbing with language. She hardly noticed the loss of her hearing. And as the river gushed joy around their light-headed bodies, Angie and Moses were married.

Justine Vogenthaler

JUSTINE VOGENTHALER, who is late-deafened, lives in Chicago, Illinois. She grew up with auditory dyslexia and has since lost her hearing. Her poems mirror her experiences as a woman who grew up with auditory challenges.

Between Two Worlds

I've never belonged,
Not fully.
Not in the deaf world,
not in the hearing world,
Not fully.
No one understands,
She does.
The clatter and clank,
The rancor, the rage.
She does.
Meaningless sounds all blending together.
Forever separating me one from another.
No one entering the place I reside.
She does.
Side by side,
reaching out,
never in.
Pulling this way and that,
wearing me thin.
I cringe,
with the thought of each new day.
Always, stretching and fetching,
bits of this and that.
A gesture here,
a word there.
This person's expression.
That person's mention.
Sweet Jesus,
Where does it end!?
She understands.
I seek for that connection.
The phone is a poorly contrived compromise.

Letters take far too long to arrive.
Yet, somehow we survive.
While living our separate lives.
She understands,
We understand,
I understand.
Time passes like sand through a sieve,
we give.
She is **deaf?**
I am **not?**
She understands,
I understand.
We have brought well-fought understanding to each other's lives,
each other's strivings, fumblings and bumblings.
We understand each other as no other can.
I am not hearing,
She is not deaf.
She is she,
I am me.
She is me and I am she.
We are one in the Whole,
a part of the ONE.
One in the Same.

Cicadas Roar

Cicadas roar
Making me oh so very sore
Making such an infernal tour of every nerve
Serve no purpose or reason
Perhaps one season
Long ago
They served a rhyme or reason for ringing in my ear
I wish I could understand what they are trying to sing
Some meaningless out of key tune
That forever rings
Morning, noon and night
In ears that grow weaker with every passing year

2 Triple Ought

(a play on numbers and words)

I just got used to writing
Two triple ought/
2000
or
double ought/
'00.
Why wasn't it triple ought/
'000
?
Too many zeros.

From one triple nine.
1999.
or
double nine
'99.
Why wasn't it triple nine
'999
?

Soon it will be two double ought one
2001,
or
ought one.
'01.
Why won't it be double ought one?
Or
'001
?

Did the millennium start at two triple ought

?

Or

Will it at two double ought one

?

We really 0 2 know?

It's all so academic.

Who cares about all the ought two's?

0'n we just be?
Time is a random act of measurement any ways.

Willy Conley

Willy Conley of Hanover, Maryland, is a professional actor, director, photographer, and award-winning playwright whose plays have been produced nationally and abroad. Some of Conley's writings and photographs were published in Gallaudet University Press's *No Walls of Stone*, an anthology of literature by deaf and hard of hearing writers. His article "From Lipreading Ants to Flying Over Cuckoo Nests" about Deaf theatre artists was featured in the April 2001 issue of *American Theatre*. He also wrote two chapters on deaf theatre for the NYU Press Deaf Studies reader, *Deaf World*. Conley holds a Master of Arts degree in Playwriting from Boston University, where he studied under Nobel Laureate Derek Walcott, and a Master of Fine Arts in Theatre from Towson University. Currently, he is an associate professor of Theatre Arts at Gallaudet University in Washington, D.C., while maintaining his status as an Associate Artist with Center Stage and an Affiliate Artist with Quest: Arts for Everyone.

Every Man Must Fall

The E.R.

We frequently get called to the E.R. to photograph the following cases: rape, child abuse, wife beating, and police brutality. You MUST shoot the injured areas and the face in the same photo. When shooting, vary the flash angle to reveal the bumps, bruises, and cuts. Be sure to shoot lots of pictures—it would be disastrous to under-shoot when it comes to medical-legal situations. Each slide must be hand-labeled with your signature and date on the back in case you get called to court to testify that you were the photographer on the case. Hand deliver the photos to the requesting physician and have him sign your log to show proof that the images were delivered. NEVER give the photos to a lawyer, a patient, or a police officer; they must ask the physician for copies.

WHEN MAX WAS told what the announcement over Dulaney High's public address system was all about—that his friend, Billy Hendricks, had drowned in the Loch Raven Reservoir, all he could do was sit there and stare at the wooden speaker above the door. How could such tragic news spill through the speaker's fabric screen and yet nothing could be seen coming out. Max was of a world where all information had to come to him visually. Most of his classmates and teachers never understood that, despite repeated attempts to explain the realities of his deafness.

Minutes before Max learned of the tragedy, the sun was shining bright and cheerful rays into the classroom. Morning announcements went on dreadfully long, and to him they sounded like an alley dog barking incessantly. Since he couldn't lipread dogs and knew dogs couldn't enunciate anything better than an "arf," "yap," or "rowf," Max ignored the morning cacophony and killed time playing tic-tac-toe tournaments with Flathead, his desk-neighbor.

Flathead used condoms with see-through packages for "O's" while Max put down twisted paper clips for "X's." The tourney winner would get a six-pack of beer. Flathead was about to drop an "O" to win a game when he suddenly stopped midway, pressing the condom between his fingers. He looked up at the doorway. Max could tell he was listening to the speaker by the way he tilted his head. Max imagined that if Flathead turned at the proper angle, a stream of words would enter cleanly into his ear, like water through a funnel. Max envied him for getting information that easily.

Flathead put the condom down and bowed his head. Max saw students behind him talking rapidly to each other. Others sat quietly, wide-eyed and slack-jawed. A few of the girls began to weep. One girl got up and walked hurriedly out of the classroom. Max looked over to Mr. Crumwell, his homeroom teacher, for some visual reference. Crumwell looked up towards the speaker, shook his head in disgust, mumbled something that looked like "he asked for it", and went back to grading papers. Somebody in the senior class must've gotten caught in the lavatory for smoking pot and wasn't going to be able to graduate — probably the star varsity pitcher or quarterback.

Max nudged Flathead's skinny arm. Flathead looked up at Max, all sad-eyed, running his hand over his crew top soothing himself. Max gave him a questioning gesture with an upward shake of his head asking, "What's up?"

Max knew something more serious than a pot bust had happened. Flathead didn't get emotional unless he won at tic-tac-toe or lined up a hot date for a mixer. He flipped the tic-tac-toe sheet over, grabbed the pencil and wrote, "Billy Hendricks died."

Max had to read it a few times. Flathead couldn't spell to save his life, and Max wondered if he wrote an incomplete sentence like, "Billy Hendricks did."

To confirm the spelling, Max whispered, "Are you saying Billy Hendricks d-i-e-d?"

Mr. Crumwell and the students in the front of the class suddenly turned their heads to look at Max. He thought he had whispered.

Flathead's lips quivered. He scrawled the words, "drowned, lock ravin."

It was then that Desson Maxwell, otherwise known as Max, took the good hard look at the loudspeaker with the coarse fabric covering its front, wishing that somehow captions could come out of it during announcements. Perhaps no one would think this was such a big deal but Max wanted the right to get the news at the same time as everyone else, especially news concerning some-one he cared about.

This was the first experience with death that had affected Max. When one of the boys in his Cub Scout troop, a kid with asthma, had died, it had not shaken him. The kid was a snob. Only a year ahead of him in elementary school, the boy always acted like he was more intelligent and talented. Max felt as if the kid perceived him as retarded and suspected it was because of his deafness. Max didn't know why the kid thought he was such hot shit because whenever the troop played baseball, the kid had to take a whiff from his inhaler thing between empty swings at the plate. And here was Max whiffling balls over the stone wall in left field, rounding the bases as easy as breathing in his sleep.

One October evening at home, Max was helping his mother carve out a pumpkin in preparation for a Scout meeting. She was the troop's den mother. His mother received a phone call that brought tears to her eyes. He was told later that the call was about the asthmatic troop member. The kid simply couldn't get enough oxygen and had died the previous day. How could anyone not have enough air? There's so much of it outside. Max asked his mother about this later but she shrugged him off and dabbed her eyes again with a Kleenex. Now this one he really couldn't figure out. The kid wasn't her son.

Max approached Mr. Crumwell and asked to be excused. He was feeling all knotty inside and needed some air and water. Thankfully, there wasn't anybody in the lavatory. He didn't know what he was going to feel, but whatever it was, he wanted to feel it alone without anyone scrutinizing his facial expressions or listening to sounds he might make. He clogged the drain with some papers towels and turned on the cold water to fill the sink up to the overflow level. He lowered his face into the water until numbness from the cold came over him. He tried to envision what Billy's face must've looked like under water. Bloated? White? Smiling? Yawning, maybe?

Max couldn't believe his buddy was killed by a substance so weak and insubstantial as water — dead from the very thing he worked with. Billy and Max worked side-by-side as dishwashers on Saturdays and Sundays at the White Coffee Pot, a family restaurant nestled between Read's Drugstore and Hardware Fair in a strip shopping center. Billy was the kind of guy who would probably grow up to be a Klan member or the president of the local chapter of the NRA. His blazing orange hair matched a hunter's outdoor shirt, and a badly chipped front tooth gave him a smile that showed you something was missing. Although he was only seventeen years old, he had the belly of a beer drinker.

After six months of working together at the White Coffee Pot, Billy got fired. Max found out why when Sylvia, the manager, called him out of the kitchen and had him sit across from her in one of the black Naugahyde booths. She stared at him a long time before saying a word. Max mentally ran through a list of all the things that he shouldn't have done in the back: dipping his fingers in the cornbread batter, taking crab cakes home, squirting the dishwasher hose at a waitress's legs, or neglecting to mop the floor on the late nights when he was tired and alone.

Over-enunciating a bit for his benefit, Sylvia asked, "Have you ever looked down into the women's restroom?" When she said "down" her jaw dropped low enough for him to see that she had spent a lot of time in a dental office getting her teeth filled with gold.

"Looked down? I'm sorry, I don't know what you're talking about."

"You've never, ever looked down in the women's restroom??"

"The only time I even look in there is when I empty the trash can and mop the floor after we close. What happened?"

"You honestly don't know?" She put her index finger to her head to emphasize the word "know" in hopes that it might rouse his memory. The gesture made Max feel like he was deaf-and-dumb.

"No ma'am," he said, using his best speech. "I swear." During this line of questioning, he leaned forward on the table and stroked his chin. He had read in a book about body language that this posture would show that he was seriously thinking about what the other person was saying. Max hid his other hand under the table, keeping it busy exploring hardened pieces of bubble gum, nuts and bolts, a carved-out hole.... Then, finally he grasped what she was asking.

Once Billy had invited him up in the rafters to take a peek in the Ladies' Room. He said he cut out a small hole in the corner of the ceiling — small enough that no one inside could really notice it but large enough so that someone outside could see everything that went on inside. Virtuously, he told Billy he wasn't interested. Max tried to sound cool and not so hard-up to see female anatomy. Actually, he made a note to himself to check it out one day when he was the sole dishwasher on a weekend. The very next time he worked alone, an opportunity presented itself. The restaurant was closed and it was just him, Esther the cook, and a couple of waitresses cleaning up. Esther was about 40, with a pockmarked face and a body pushing against an extra-large cook's uniform. She put down her grill scrub brush and apron, and headed for the back.

Max quickly went over to the walk-in refrigerator pretending to stock up on "prep" foods for the next day. He timed opening the refrigerator just as Esther opened the door to the Ladies' Room. He closed the walk-in quietly without going inside and went up the ladder.

There were greasy hand prints on the ceiling tiles where Billy had pushed them aside to gain access. Max's heart was beating fast since he wouldn't be able to hear if one of the waitresses came by. He put his hand up to the same corner where Billy's hand prints were found, noticing that Billy's hands were smaller than his. Amazing how an ego exaggerated one's size.

Cartons of lettuce, tomatoes, and potatoes were down below the ladder waiting to be stored in the walk-in. Max looked once more at the ceiling tile, paused, and then came back down the ladder. He had enough of a stigma being deaf. If caught, he would never get another job in his entire life. He visualized the rumors that would spread about the incompetencies and sexual vagaries of the deaf.

Across from him in the booth Sylvia lit up a filterless Pall Mall. She politely bent her head down to spit out some loose tobacco strands in the direction of her lap. Each "spphht" was followed by a puff of smoke.

"Well, I just fired Mr. Hendricks for lewd behavior in the back." She drew a heavy sigh and exhaled another column of smoke.

"Oh, really?" He stifled the urge to grab a napkin from the dispenser to tear apart and roll up into little balls to calm his nerves.

"I went in the back the other day to check out how many crab cakes we had left in the walk-in."

"Y-yeah," he answered, not sure if she was asking him a question.

"Well, I saw where that ladder was when I came out of the walk-in. Mr. Hendricks was standing on it, half up in the ceiling looking down into the women's restroom."

"Oh my God," said Max, slapping his forehead to demonstrate disapproval.

Sylvia ended her interrogation the same way she had opened it, with an eagle-eyed stare. He was innocent, of course, but he was afraid that his knowledge of the hole would trip this human lie detector. Finally, Sylvia put out her cigarette in the white ashtray shaped like a coffee pot and slid out of the booth. Max grabbed a napkin and quickly rolled a couple of little paper balls between his fingertips before going back to the dishes.

At school, Billy and Max happened to be in the same photography class. Billy said he took photography to get out of his art requirement. He couldn't stand the idea of sitting on a stool for two hours slapping paint onto a canvas; that was for girls, and boys who wanted to be girls.

Since there weren't enough darkrooms to go around, they shared one. Billy picked Max for a partner because of Max's premature baldness. To Billy's mind, that meant Max was the most mature student around who wouldn't give a flick about what was said or done. Besides, Max was deaf and pretty much kept to himself. All Billy wanted to do was read *Playboy* magazines under the seedy illumination of a safelight.

Max ended up doing Billy's black-and-white prints. In exchange, Billy worked at the restaurant in Max's place any time he needed a Saturday or Sunday off to spend with his girlfriend who lived an hour and a half away.

Filling in at the restaurant wasn't the only reason why Max was willing to develop Billy's prints. The fat sucker had a damn good eye for composition and God only knew where he got it from. Billy's mother ran the laundromat at the end of the shopping center. All she did was open the place, made sure nobody walked out with a washer or dryer, locked up at closing time, and hurried home to watch *Dialing for Dollars* by the telephone. His father worked for the highway department filling pot holes and striping yellow lines on the streets of Baltimore. He also ran the plow and salt truck during the winter when it snowed. His parents definitely didn't seem to carry any genes for a good eye in photographic composition.

In the most ordinary subjects Billy found something extraordinary — like he'd shoot a rusty nail on a barn door. Big funky deal, right? In the developer bath, that 8 x 10-inch print came out looking like a Walker Evans or Dorothea Lange masterpiece from the Depression era. Max's pictures always ended up looking like cliches; the proverbial sunset smack dab in the middle of a print with the requisite seagull silhouetted against the sky.

Billy used his grandfather's old Leica range finder, the kind where you looked through the viewfinder from the upper left corner of the camera. Max didn't know how Billy did it since range finders never recorded exactly what was seen through the glass. Max's pictures were always off-center whenever he shot with that kind of camera.

When Billy went shooting, he "burned" film. He'd shoot up a roll of 36 exposures on that one rusty nail whereas Max hated to waste more than two frames on a subject.

"Billy, where did you learn to shoot like that?" Max would ask.

"Nowheres. I just aim and click, is all."

"But, there's more to it than that. I mean, how did you come up with stuff like taking pictures of water reflections and then turning the photos upside down to make your images look like the real thing?"

"Shit-if-I-know, man," Billy would say, holding his *Playboy* centerfold up vertically for a minute.

"I've never seen anybody turn their reflections upside-down. That's ingenious! You're a regular Monet, painting with your camera."

"What're you talking about money for?" he asked.

"Mo – nay."

"What is it? Some kind of an eel or sumthin'?" Then, he would give Max that chipped-tooth smile.

Max suspected Billy knew he was an artist but would never let on to anyone. Art was for faggots and for some reason Billy had a backwoods, tobacco-chewing reputation to maintain.

After the day Billy was fired, Max didn't see him much. He stopped going to photography classes. His blue, souped-up '62 Valiant with the small Confederate flag on the aerial was rarely seen about town. Max missed Billy's brazen presence but was so caught up in the end-of-the-year school activities that he almost forgot about Billy—until the morning of the death announcement.

Several months after Billy died, Max went fishing for old time's sake at the Loch Raven Reservoir under a Fourth of July sky that was as blue as it could ever get. He stood in the water up to his knees, holding the line of his bamboo rod out by the deep pocket where he knew sunfish liked to hang out. Max kept an eye on the red and white bobber waiting for it to be pulled under. He and Billy used to troll in the area of Goetze's Cove for sunfish on Fourth of July weekends when they got time off from work. Whenever a catfish snatched onto Billy's line, he ripped the hook out of its mouth, replaced it with a lit firecracker, and heaved it in the air to explode like a grenade.

"What did you do that for, Bill?"

"Doin' my part for wildlife conservation."

"Man, you're a piece of wildlife. What's your part?"

"Keepin' the ugly fish population down. It's a bottom-feeder. You ever ate one of them?"

"No."

"Tastes like a dirty dishrag from all that shit it sucks up from the lake bottom."

"Yeah, right, Bill, I guess you would know the flavor of dirty dishrags."

Up on the bank of the cove was the granite, big as an old one-door refrigerator laying on its side. Max always thought of it as Billy's rock. According to the local news, this was near where Billy's body was pulled out of the water. It was at the rock that Max first saw Billy, after moving to the area. A small crowd of kids by the granite were yelling at Billy not to do whatever it was he was doing. He was a skinny little runt then. As Max snuck in for a closer view, he saw Billy pounding something against the rock over and over – a box turtle with its shell cracked apart and blood dripping out. Besides this pre-pubescent act of violence, what also stunned Max was the cloud-colored, gelatinous remains of the tortoise. He never realized turtles had a lump of jelly under their shells. And there was Billy grinning at this wondrous discovery, his eyes sparkling in the late afternoon sun. Max couldn't remember if his friend had the chip in his tooth then. In later years, Billy claimed he held his secret M.P.A. club meetings at the rock.

"What's M.P.A. stand for, Bill?"

"I ain't gonna tell you. You ain't a member."

Max wondered if Billy's club had any members at all. One of the neighborhood kids told Max in confidence that M.P.A. stood for Mashed Potatoes Association. It wasn't until the time when Billy and Max worked together at the White Coffee Pot that the potato connection was made. Billy craved mashed potatoes with a crater of butter and always kept a plate of them on the side while washing dishes.

The bobber continued to float in place, the white half still above the water. About three feet away, an object underwater reflected the sunlight. Max tried to edge toward it but kept slipping on smooth algae-covered rocks. He didn't want some crayfish snapping at his toes. If Billy was looking down on him at that moment and knew his thoughts, he would think that was awful sissified of him. In his head, he gave Billy the finger.

Max lowered the bamboo pole and tried to probe the object. Attached to it was a dark strap wavering in the water. Max caught the strap with the pole and retracted it. The strap slid off. He dipped the pole under and fished for the strap again. The object felt heavy and metallic as Max finally pulled it up.

It was a Leica range finder. Max swung the pole over and eased the camera on the bank. After cleaning the mud off, he could see that the film's counter was on "13." The rewind knob was taut indicating that there was indeed film inside. He took the camera home and kept it submerged in a sink of water to preserve the film until it could be brought to school the next morning for processing.

Not many people were at the photo lab since it was summer school. In the darkroom Max got the absurd feeling that if he opened the camera back, minnows would flop out, but all that did was musty water. He developed the film and after fifteen minutes turned the lights on. The moldy smell was replaced by the vinegary odor of photographic chemicals. He washed the film and held it up to the bare bulb overhead. Twelve frames had been exposed of somebody's face, all looking similar, perhaps a man's face — hard to tell since these were negative images. The film was dried, cut into strips, and put into protective sleeves. Max took out a strip and inserted it into the enlarger.

He cranked the enlarger to blow the image up to an 8 x 10 size. He made an exposure and slipped the print into the developer. As he rocked the tray back and forth to agitate the chemicals, the image of Billy appeared on the paper. He wasn't smiling, yawning, or giving that devil-may-care look of his. The look was more like a downed U.S. fighter pilot held as a P.O.W. during the Viet Nam War. Billy's right eye was black and swollen shut. Across his forehead was a caterpillar-shaped gash. His nose had the unmistakable curve of a break in the middle. A thin but deep-looking cut on his chin showed that he was probably knifed. Both cheeks were swollen. His good eye looked dead-dull.

Max's heart rate became rapid and his throat went dry. He leaned over the darkroom sink and drank water from the faucet. He took the print out of the developer and bathed it in the other chemicals before continuing to wash the image of Billy Hendricks. Even though he was dead, Max felt comforted by the thought that he was cleansing Billy's wounds. Maybe no one was able to do this for him at the time. But what happened? Did Billy take these himself on a self-timer or did some bruiser shoot the pictures to record his handiwork and forgot to take the film out? Max couldn't tell from the background where the photos were taken. It was all white, probably a wall by the way the shadows fell behind Billy.

More prints were made from the rest of the negatives. All turned out basically the same except that the angles were slightly different in each frame. One shot was a little tilted. Another a little higher. A third, a bit to the left, and so forth. But, in all of them, Billy had that straight-ahead dead stare at the lens. It was a look Max had never seen in any of Billy's most mischievous moments.

Max cleaned and dried up everything in the darkroom. He decided not to show the prints to anyone in the lab, and walked home contemplating what to do with this newfound evidence. He didn't want to take the pictures to Billy's parents, suspicious that Billy's father might be involved in this somehow. Billy and his father never got on and often wound up having fistfights in their backyard. Billy once said that when his old man got older, he was going to do to him what he had done to the turtle—crack the old man's skull and expose the jelly underneath that tough exterior.

If Max went to the cops, they'd go into some full-blown investigation probing into everybody's lives and turning everything upside-down. Max resisted the need to show the pictures to people because he was well aware of their fickle nature of blabbing away secrets.

Fortunately, Max's parents weren't home yet. He pushed his mother's plants aside on the windowsill and opened the kitchen window. He moved the dirty dishes and glasses out of the sink and set them on the counter. He lifted the negatives and prints out of the box and set them by the sink. The soft light coming through the window made Billy look more vulnerable. It made him think of that song, *I Shall Be Released*, they always sang at Young Life meetings during junior high school. Max never really associated its meaning with anything until now, although he assumed they were singing about Jesus Christ after he read the lyrics his mother wrote down for him. "They say every man needs protection...they say that every man must fall." He felt all knotty again in his eyes and throat.

Max got a box of wooden matches out of the drawer and struck one. Suspending the prints and negatives over the sink, he held the match up to the corner of the photos, watching the flame grow big. The papers curled and the plastic sizzled. On the 8 x 10, the black around Billy's swollen eye grew bigger until it was black all over. Just when Max could no longer stand the heat, he dropped the images in the sink and waited until they were reduced to ashes. He brushed the soot down the drain and put in the drain plug. Turning on the hot water and squeezing in some detergent, he transferred the dirty tableware back into the sink. Then grabbing a sponge Max began to wash the dishes.

Salt in the Basement

An American Sign Language Reverie in English

me little, almost high wash-wash machine
down basement, me have blue car
drive drive round round
basement

happen summer
me inside blue car
drive round round
basement

me drive every corner
drive drive drive
then BOOM! me crash

there brown paper round tall
me get out car
look inside brown round tall
many many small small
white rock rock
small white rock rock

for-for?

me put white rock rock
in mouth
very very salty
same-same Grandma
mashed-mashed potato

me again sit blue car
drive round round
basement

happen winter
father down basement
go to brown round tall
father shovel big lump
there white rock rock
many white rock rock

father told me for-for
outside road

me ask again for-for?

me outside blue car, cold cold
drive drive straight straight
me watch father

white rock rock father throw throw
on walk-walk
father his brown car
throw white rock rock
throw round throw round

me ask father for-for?

father say for mother
white rock rock for mother?

me get off blue car
me look down white rock rock
burn burn hole many many
hole in ice
same-same ice my lemon drink

me jaw-drop
white rock rock
make hole in ice break-break
same-same make hole in my tummy?

that why me pee-pee
poo-poo always?

me no more eat
white rock rock
down basement

me remember
mother year past
happen winter
mother outside
ice all-over
mother fall
arm broke

father told me
go down basement
stay stay
me inside blue car
drive round round
basement

The Cycle of the X-Ray Technician

Whenever I feel down about my deafness,
my receding hairline, my weight,
my glaucoma, and on and on, I remind myself —
the X-Ray technician.

I passed him every time I delivered
some files to medical records.
He'd hang up recently-processed X-Rays
on the light boxes with the blue light
illuminating a badly-burned and disfigured face —
the X-Ray technician.

He had one normal arm,
the other a prosthesis with a metal "claw."
I'd start to feel sorry for him
then I stopped myself.
I wouldn't want him to pity me —
the X-Ray technician.

For all I know, he may have his own home
with a beautiful wife, lover or family.
He may be an excellent artist
or a reputable auto mechanic.
He may be the best bowler in Texas
or have the highest R.B.I.'s on his softball team
or, he may be lonely,
feeling sorry for himself like me —
the X-Ray technician. . . .

The Perfect Woman

At least once a day
on the balcony of his small-town loft
he leans against the railing
watching
the cars go by

His gaze would shift across the street
to a fancy country store
with an antique wedding dress
yellowing
in the display window

It is twilight and the dress
hanging
glows white under the track lights

He feels he is
wasting
his entire life waiting

Tonya Marie Stremlau

Tonya Marie Stremlau was born and raised in New Orleans, Louisiana. She became deaf at age 10 from spinal meningitis. She received an M.A. in English from the University of Nebraska-Lincoln and a Ph.D. in English, with a specialization in composition and rhetoric, from Louisiana State University. She now lives in Maryland and is an associate professor in the English Department of Gallaudet University. Her favorite courses to teach are any that involve teaching writing and deaf people in literature. It is the best job in the world since she not only gets to work with deaf students but with reading and writing, which she also does for fun. Her other favorite free-time activities are cooking and taking long walks, whether alone to think or with a friend to chat.

A Nice Romantic Dinner

SARA, SITTING ON THE bench in the warm evening sun outside of her favorite Cajun restaurant in Washington, D.C., looked at her watch. It said 6:30, so Brad was now 30 minutes late; because it was a weeknight, they had agreed to come straight from their respective jobs and meet at the restaurant. Since Sara drove and Brad took Metro, they would be able to go home together. She wasn't worried, Brad was frequently late, but she was annoyed. Sara had actually gotten there a little early, partly out of excitement—Sara and Brad were celebrating their seventh anniversary—and partly because she was anal about being on time. After seven years she should have known that Brad would be late, and resolved (not for the first time) to start telling him that she wanted to meet or leave at least 15 minutes before she really did. She never followed through on these resolutions, however, sure that the first time she did, Brad would actually show up then and use it against her.

As Sara waited, she thought back to seven years ago. Sara and Brad had had a whirlwind courtship; they became engaged after two months of dating and married six months after that. They had both fallen in love quickly and hard, and getting married had seemed like the logical thing to do. That way they could pursue together the life they imagined—graduate school, then jobs and two or three kids. Sara was used to men being turned off or intimidated by her competitiveness and intellect if they weren't already scared off by the fact that she was deaf.

The wedding had been nice—simple but nice. It had mostly gone right. It rained, but they were inside. The cake leaned, but it didn't fall. Brad forgot to pick up the ice for the drinks, but Sara's brothers went out to get it. Sara's mom complained that Sara's dress was too low cut, but Sara's aunts said it was gorgeous. And, best of all for Sara, for the first time she had a sign language interpreter while she was with her extended family; at last, she was able to talk easily to her grandparents and aunts and uncles and cousins.

Sara came back to the present when she saw Brad walking toward the restaurant. He was easy to pick out from a distance because he was tall and had a distinctive, bouncy walk. His blond hair (thinning some now that he was in his early 30s) also made him easy to pick out. He hadn't noticed her yet, so she got up, waved, and walked to meet him. He was carrying a bouquet of red and white carnations, her favorite flower. Sara's annoyance at Brad for being late melted some, and she reached up to give him a kiss. "You are late," she said and signed. "Let's go eat!"

"Happy Anniversary," he said, and gave her the flowers.

The hostess led them through the dining area. Since it was a Tuesday evening, there weren't too many people eating dinner. Fewer than half of the tables were occupied. The décor left no doubt that the cuisine was Cajun: Mardi Gras posters, a mural of a swamp scene with a big alligator, a collection of hot sauce bottles. Sara and Brad were seated at a table near the right wall. Sara sat where she could see the whole restaurant, with her back to the wall; she liked to be able to see what everyone else was doing since she couldn't hear them. The alligator's head in the mural was directly over hers, a reptilian guardian angel, sure to scare off any undesirables.

The hostess gave them their menus and left them alone. Sara opened her menu and started reading through. Decisions, decisions. How to order when just about everything looks good? Etouffee? Catfish? Half-and-half fried oysters and crawfish? If oysters really had an aphrodisiac effect, that might be a good anniversary meal.

She was still reading through the descriptions of the various entrees when out of the corner of her eye she saw a waiter standing next to the table and looked up. The waiter was already in mid-sentence of whatever it was he was saying, so Sara looked at Brad for him to tell her what the waiter was saying. She caught his eye and raised her eyebrows quizzically but Brad didn't say anything until she kicked him under the table. The specials of the evening were oyster stew and lobster stuffed with crab and topped with crawfish etouffee.

Sara decided that, as good as the lobster sounded, she would go with her old favorite. She pointed at her menu to let the waiter know that she wanted the crawfish etouffee and a bottle of Abita Amber. She didn't catch whatever it was Brad told the waiter he wanted. The candlelight made it even harder than usual to see what people were saying. The "romantic" dinner atmosphere was hardly prime lipreading territory. Sara wished very hard that Brad would learn sign, if only to make times like this easier. Then Brad said something she missed, and got up and headed toward the bathroom. She figured he had said that he wanted to wash his hands because he always went to wash his hands before eating. After seven years, there weren't many surprises.

The waiter brought their drinks before Brad came back—two bottles of Abita Amber and two glasses. Sara ignored her glass and began sipping her beer from the bottle. When Brad sat down again, Sara said, "While we are waiting for our food to come, why don't I teach you a few signs?" Brad didn't look too enthusiastic, but he didn't refuse, either, so Sara went ahead, rearranging the objects on the table to make the lesson easier. To force Brad to really use his eyes, to see the words, she would do a basic object-sign connection instead of giving him the English equivalent. She had theorized lately that Brad wasn't learning the signs she had tried to teach him because he was still using his ears instead of his eyes.

She arranged, from her right to left across the table the salt and pepper shakers, the little box with packets of sugar, Sweet-n-Low, and Equal, her empty glass and partially full beer bottle (she left his alone), and her silverware still wrapped in a rose-colored cloth napkin.

Brad had turned and was looking toward the bar, so Sara tapped on the table to get his attention. When he looked over, she smiled and picked up the salt and pepper shakers, salt in her right hand, pepper in the left, held them up, and nodded to Brad. He nodded back, so Sara figured that he was following her. She put them down, pointed at the salt shaker, and signed "salt." Brad looked at her and said "salt." Sara wanted him to repeat the sign, not just the English word (because she thought that doing so would help him remember the sign) so she nodded her head but repeated the sign and then gestured for him to copy. He looked frustrated, but he attempted to imitate her. His sign was awkward, but it approximated the actual sign, so Sara smiled and gave him a thumbs-up.

She repeated the operation to teach the signs for pepper, beer, bottle, glass, knife, fork, spoon, and napkin. None of these signs should have been new to Brad; not only had Sara given similar lessons at previous meals, but Brad had completed a course in ASL I (although he missed several classes and—as far as Sara knew—did no practicing except when she demanded it). From Brad's responses, though, it looked like he didn't remember ever having seen any of the signs before. Sara tried very hard to stay patient, but inside she felt like screaming.

The waiter brought some French bread, butter, and an appetizer. "Fried alligator," Brad said. Sara smiled because it was a special treat, and she hadn't had any alligator for over a year. She hadn't ordered an appetizer herself because she had been planning to save room for dessert—the restaurant had a very good bread pudding with rum sauce—but what the hell. "Fried alligator," she signed back to Brad, and took a bit and popped it in her mouth.

Instead of repeating what she had signed, Brad said, "That's enough for now. My eyes are tired, and it is dark in here. Let's just talk and eat." He picked up his beer and closed his eyes while he drank several swallows, giving Sara no chance to argue with him. "Bastard!" Sara signed (but did not voice). Brad missed it, of course, since his eyes were closed. Not that it would matter anyway; Sara doubted Brad knew that particular sign.

Sara was furious. Brad had the nerve to complain that it was too dark in the restaurant to pay attention to her sign, and he wanted her to pay attention to his lips, which are infinitely harder to understand? She was struggling not to cry, not wanting to make a scene in public.

Sara also fought the urge to run to the restroom, where she could close the door of a booth, give into the tears, and shut away the frustrating hearing world. It was time to stop running away, time to stop avoiding the problem. The last time Sara had hidden in a bathroom, she had promised herself it would be the last. Just a few weeks before, the last time Sara and Brad had been out, they had gone to the home of one of Brad's work friends for dinner because one of the work group was moving away. Sara usually tried to avoid such gatherings, but lately she had been insisting Brad join her friends more—her deaf friends—so she figured she should join him with his friends.

As usual, the group setting defeated Sara's unusually good lipreading skills. Or to be more accurate, Sara didn't even try to follow the conversation because she knew her efforts would be wasted. Sara was pretty good at occupying herself in such situations, since she had years of practice. Before dinner, while everyone was making small talk in the living room, Sara played with the household cat, a very friendly orange tabby. When everyone moved to the dining room for dinner, Sara focused on eating. The first course was salad, and since Sara was eating instead of talking she was the first to finish.

With nothing better to do, she nudged Brad and asked, "What is everyone talking about?"

"Oh, nothing much, work stuff."

Sara then gave up for the moment and studied their hostess's teapot collection displayed on a built-in shelf that ran completely around the room just above door height. Some had matching teacups and saucers. Some of the teapots were just pretty china, some were handmade pottery, and some were made to look like other things—a cottage, a cat, a little red caboose. Then Sara saw that everyone was laughing and again nudged Brad, raised her eyebrows, and gave him "the look" to fill her in on what was happening. Brad raised his hand and motioned to her to wait. Sara didn't like that, so she kicked him under the table.

When Brad still didn't tell her what everyone was talking and laughing about, she took her napkin off her lap and went off to find the bathroom. She locked herself in and remembered to turn on the vent fan. Years before, when they were newlyweds and visiting his parents, Brad had told her to always turn the vent on or everyone could hear what she was doing in the bathroom. She usually didn't care if hearing people could hear her in the bathroom and actually found it amusing that they might be offended or embarrassed. This time, though, she didn't want them to hear her because she was going to cry.

It was in that bathroom she made the decision that it was time to stop running, to stop trying to hide her discomfort so as not to bother the hearing people. So as not to embarrass Brad.

Well, those days were over. She took a sip of her beer and looked up at Brad, who looked exasperated. He rolled his eyes and pursed his lips and shook his head. He was looking at her like she was a naughty child. She knew he was thinking that she was overreacting; he probably wasn't even exactly sure why she was angry.

Sara, of course, thought she was being perfectly reasonable. The urge to cry was replaced with cold anger. She ate more of the alligator in silence, trying to ignore Brad. It was her old strategy for dealing with these times when Brad refused to work on his sign when she wanted him to: if he wouldn't sign, she wouldn't talk. She thought the message couldn't be clearer, but apparently he wasn't getting it very well.

When their dinners came, Sara focused on her plate. Her etouffee was very good, and it would be a real shame to waste it.

Brad tried to start a conversation several times, but Sara conscientiously ignored him and thought about what she could do to make Brad understand how much he hurt her. Talking to him wouldn't work; it sure hadn't all the previous times when, after a fight like this, she would explain that she was scared that if he didn't learn sign now he never would, and she would end up a stranger in her own family, unable to follow conversations between him and the children they were planning to have, and that they would end up divorced. At the moment, divorce was looking like a pretty good option.

She finished off her beer and found inspiration.

Sara tapped the table to get Brad's attention, and lifted her hands to sign. She saw Brad press his lips together, his whole expression communicating more clearly than any words that he did not want to communicate through sign, definitely not now, and maybe not ever. So Sara used one sign she was positive he knew.

"Fuck you," she signed, and left, heading to her car and home. Brad could take Metro. She figured that would give her enough time to get home, pack a few things, and leave—for the night, or forever.